Quality Management
in the
Nonprofit World

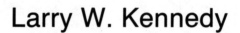

Larry W. Kennedy

Foreword by Philip Crosby

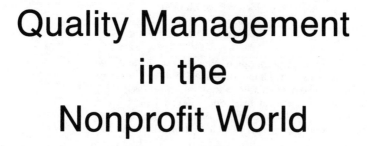

Quality Management
in the
Nonprofit World

*Combining Compassion
and Performance
to Meet Client Needs
and Improve Finances*

Jossey-Bass Publishers

San Francisco • Oxford • 1991

QUALITY MANAGEMENT IN THE NONPROFIT WORLD
Combining Compassion and Performance to Meet Client Needs and Improve Finances
by Larry W. Kennedy

Copyright © 1991 by: Jossey-Bass Inc., Publishers
       350 Sansome Street
       San Francisco, California 94104
       &
       Jossey-Bass Limited
       Headington Hill Hall
       Oxford OX3 0BW

Library of Congress Cataloging-in-Publication Data

Kennedy, Larry.
 Quality management in the nonprofit world : combining compassion and
performance to meet client needs and improve finances / Larry W.
Kennedy. — 1st ed.
   p. cm. — (Jossey-Bass nonprofit sector series)
  Includes bibliographical references and index.
  ISBN 1-55542-346-9
  1. Corporations, Nonprofit — Management. 2. Corporations,
Nonprofit — Finance. I. Title. II. Series.
HD62.6.K48 1991
658.15 — dc20   90-28986
                         CIP

Manufactured in the United States of America

The paper in this book meets the guidelines for
permanence and durability of the Committee on
Production Guidelines for Book Longevity of
the Council on Library Resources.

JACKET DESIGN BY ANNE ELDREDGE

FIRST EDITION

Code 9149

The Jossey-Bass
Nonprofit Sector Series

Contents

Foreword

Philip Crosby Associates, Inc. (PCA) is known worldwide for training for-profit companies in how to manage the quality of their work; so when we began our community relations program, the contributions part of it posed little apparent difficulty. We decided to assign 10 percent of our pretax earnings to worthy causes and to set up a committee to make the determinations. The only rules we made were: to avoid giving to churches, since we felt that their members should take care of them, and to try to concentrate on "real people helping real people." When there was only a small amount of money involved, this was not difficult. As our budget grew, however, we were besieged by charities, all worthwhile. It became very difficult to know exactly what to do.

I had known Larry Kennedy when he was an associate pastor at our church. We had many informal discussions about the world of business and how one could be a Christian and still have a successful venture. When Larry decided to apply his skills as a consultant to the nonprofit world, we asked him to advise the contributions committee. In short order, he had us defining our objectives in clearer terms and also allocating a percentage of funds for each of the different areas of need. In this way, we would not wind up giving all our money to the arts while neglecting children or emphasizing education to the detriment of the homeless.

Larry investigated each applicant and helped us determine which were doing what they said they were. In the process of accomplishing all this, it became apparent that very few of these organizations were being managed to their potential. The people in charge were usually those dedicated to the cause involved, and they spent their time and what money came in on what was pertinent at the moment. Because of our concern for the non-profit sector, we funded Larry's efforts to help these groups get their work in order. As part of that outreach, we established special classes at the Quality College and invited the administrators to attend. This helped them gain a better understanding of the requirements of management. Larry attended all of the classes and also became a certified instructor.

While all this was going on, Larry was working on his advanced degree and beginning to outline the contents of this book in his mind. He felt, and I agreed, that the nonprofit world was sometimes looked at as not being real management. However, nothing was different in terms of defining requirements, training people, and satisfying customers. In fact, the obligations of nonprofit management teams to the people they serve are much more real and demanding than those of a for-profit organization.

This book makes a great contribution to the field of management because it puts forth a clear understanding of a much neglected subject. It also lays out the actions and concepts necessary for successful operation. Because the author is experienced in the "trenches" of nonprofit operations, the book has the ring of truth and reality. Charitable organizations that have been helped by PCA have always taken time to express their gratitude for the money they received. However, most of their comments have been in appreciation of the educational and consulting services made available to them through Larry and the Quality College.

I believe *Quality Management in the Nonprofit World* will make a significant contribution to the appreciation of management development in the nonprofit sector. We at PCA, and I personally, are very proud to have been given the opportunity to witness its development.

Winter Park, Florida   Philip Crosby
February 1991   *Founder*
                                 Philip Crosby Associates, Inc.

Preface

All of us in the nonprofit world — those who do the work and those who fund it — are pursuing that special sense of quality we experience when we effectively and specifically fulfill our objectives. It is the lure of quality that sustains us when we encounter the disappointment, rejection, loneliness, and frustration that sometimes come when we are trying to do good with our time, talents, and resources. The lessons of *Quality Management in the Nonprofit World* are intended to provide the reader with the philosophical and management tools necessary to systematically achieve quality in his or her efforts.

In the for-profit world, there are hundreds of texts that have been written to enable managers to be successful in their enterprises. However, the literature specifically targeted to process management in a nonprofit environment is almost nonexistent. The vast majority of what is written for the nonprofit world focuses on initial organizational documents, fund-raising, or accounting. There is some literature relating to strategic planning and marketing, and although a few of these texts may be helpful, they do very little to foster the overall improvement of processes and services.

The purpose of *Quality Management in the Nonprofit World* is to help individuals involved with nonprofit organizations provide their clients and constituents with services of the highest possible quality and improve the financial condition of their organizations. My intent is to empower nonprofit organizations, their contributors, and their volunteers to improve their efforts through the application of quality management principles.

Intended Audience

Quality Management in the Nonprofit World was written for all people involved in the management of nonprofit organizations. It was also written for the individual contributors and corporate grantmakers who fund work by nonprofits and who want to know which organizations they should support and how to evaluate their performance. It is also intended for the volunteers who provide nonprofits with countless hours of help and want to know more about how and where they can effectively invest their time.

Whether the reader is a trustee, executive, or staff member; a member of the clergy (as pastor, administrator, or layperson); an individual or corporate contributor; or a volunteer at any level of service — the pursuit of quality should ultimately result in the delivery of effective, practical, and compassionate services in appropriate measures to people in need.

Theoretical Background

On the topic of quality management, there are two names that stand above the rest. Philip Crosby and W. Edwards Deming have become internationally known for their expertise in quality management. Deming is known worldwide for his management prowess and has been a guiding force behind the industrial advances in Japan. Deming's consulting and managerial abilities are legend, but it took someone like Phil Crosby to sift through the concepts of quality management and bring them to a level that most people can understand.

In *Quality Is Free* (1979) and *Quality Without Tears* (1984), Crosby has ordered the concepts of quality management into clearly understandable principles that can be applied in many environments. He is able to take us beyond the engineer's perspective into the realities of business and enterprise. His application of quality management principles in banking, travel, and numerous other service industries has been revolutionary. Because of my experience as an engineer in America's space program, a businessman, and a nonprofit manager, I could see the potential of quality management, and I wanted to continue that revolution into the nonprofit world. *Quality Management in the Nonprofit World* adapts quality management principles to a nonprofit environment.

Implementing Principles into Practice

At the heart of Philip Crosby's model of quality management is what he calls the "Four Absolutes." They are principles or concepts that answer the following four questions:

1. What is quality?
2. What system is needed to cause quality?
3. What performance standard should be used?
4. What measurement system is required?

It might sound too simple to learn four principles and change the way you experience quality. Actually, if you did not already have ideas in your mind that seem the same but are patently different, it would be just that simple. Adapting quality management principles to a nonprofit environment requires us to look closely at what makes the nonprofit world tick. In each of the chapters where the absolutes are explained, I will spend considerable time describing what they are not. I have used stories to help you picture the wrong ways and the right ways to integrate the principles of quality into the special circumstances of nonprofit management. Do not be too surprised. When Philip Crosby undertook the task of teaching people in the for-profit world about quality management, he had to teach them what it was not. Preconceptions, prejudices, and predispositions are not unique to any part of society or business.

There is a natural sequence to studying the principles of quality management that I have found is particularly important to the nonprofit sector. I have separated the four absolutes into two categories: three operating principles, and a way to measure one's progress. Absolute Four focuses on the measurement of quality and what it costs when we do not do things the way they should be done. The measurement of quality is rooted in financial and human values that are very important in non-profit work. They are so important that you will learn about them first.

Overview of the Contents

In Chapter One, I explain the extraordinary human, organizational, and financial benefits of quality management and discuss important fundamentals in the measurement of quality.

Chapters Two through Four review the three operating principles (Absolutes One, Two, and Three). I recommend that you study these chapters in sequence because they build on one another in very subtle but important ways. Chapter Two also discusses how to use the principles of quality management to identify and fulfill the requirements for an organization's mission, portfolio of services, and fund-raising. Chapter Three shows how to prevent the reoccurrence of failures in the processes that deliver services to clients and raise money for an organization's mission. In Chapter Four, I present ways to raise performance levels and establish reasonable standards for client services, suppliers, and volunteers.

Chapter Five provides a review of entrepreneurial and marketing issues for nonprofits. It reviews important concepts in nonprofit administration that will be helpful to you in initiating improvement processes and in better understanding the overall nonprofit environment as it exists in our society. This review of entrepreneurial and marketing issues will add a distinctive energy to your use of the three operating principles of quality.

We often carry with us personal, traditional, and cultural hindrances to our understanding of quality that we may not be aware of and cannot easily see. If I were to list some of them, the reader might sincerely and earnestly read the list and decide that he or she does not have "those particular problems." Many of the hindrances to quality are submerged in the myth and mystique of our culture. Chapter Six shows how to identify the presence of traditional, philosophical, cultural, and social hindrances to quality management.

In Chapter Seven, I describe some of the sources of influence that can positively and negatively affect your improve-

ment path, such as community standards and grantmakers. I
also show how to make quality choices in individual and corporate values, hire staff, select professional services, train volunteers, and manage for tomorrow.

Chapter Eight suggests how to invest your time and efforts
so that your nonprofit organization can obtain the benefits of
quality management. I also review some valuable lessons I have
learned about implementing quality management principles in
nonprofit organizations.

Sharing the Treasure

Learning about quality management will create a new excitement in your life and high hopes for your efforts as a contributor, volunteer, overseer, or staff member. The measurement
of quality will become the way you evaluate situations and make
decisions in all areas of your personal life and work. You should
feel free to share the exhilaration of what you learn. However,
it is necessary to make a distinction between person-to-person
testimonials about quality management and the sobering responsibilities of someone who wants to become a change agent.

First and foremost, you must solidly obtain and display
the treasures of quality in your own life. Keep in mind that we
are a society routinely bombarded with fads that promise treasures through diet, exercise, and other self-improvement themes.
Because of the constant disappointment created by these fads,
people are sometimes more than a little cynical about anything
that promises improvement. To achieve a change in lifestyle
and in the culture of the nonprofit organization where you contribute or work, you must be prepared to invest your time and
efforts in a rational and effective manner. I suggest that you
allow the natural sequence of *Quality Management in the Nonprofit
World* to become the structural model for obtaining quality in
your life and work. Take your time and remain steadily on
course.

Orlando, Florida   Larry W. Kennedy
February 1991

The Author

Larry W. Kennedy is a management consultant with over fifteen years of experience in the nonprofit world. His interdisciplinary background in engineering and business, together with his practical experiences as a nonprofit trustee, executive, pastor, and grantmaker, has uniquely prepared him to evaluate nonprofit operations.

Kennedy received an A.A. degree (1969) from Brevard Community College in Florida. He also received a diploma of ministerial studies (1979) from the Berean School of the Bible, a B.S. degree (1980) in psychology from Florida Southern College, an M.A. degree (1987) in human resources management from Norwich University, and a Ph.D. degree (1990) in public administration from the Union Institute.

Kennedy grew up in an aerospace environment and held responsible positions in Apollo Spacecraft Operations and Flight Crew Training as a young man. It was there he was first exposed to the disciplines of quality management. His later experiences as a salesman, manager, and business owner broadened his understanding of business and management, and he gained national recognition for his sales and marketing expertise.

Kennedy's social motivations and concern for people in need led him to work in the nonprofit sector. Beginning as a counselor and lecturer, he soon began to use his organizational and administrative talents to create educational, counseling, and human service operations for various parts of the secular and religious nonprofit community. He has trained and supervised volunteers for organizations both large (one project with over 20,000 volunteers) and small and has gained a reputation for his instinctual abilities in organizational development.

As a grantmaker, he has performed hundreds of on-site program evaluations and developed innovative approaches to grantmaking and technical assistance for recipients in a broad range of social issues. He has managed philanthropic and benevolent work on a local and national scale and has administered grants in emerging and Third World nations. In 1989 he visited the Soviet Union with U.S. foundation executives to encourage and assist Soviet citizens in the development of their private sector initiatives. He has served on the steering committees of several grantmaking associations and is active in both the southeastern and national Councils on Foundations.

Kennedy's relationship with Philip Crosby, an internationally recognized expert on quality management, has significantly influenced this work. In addition to his certification as an instructor by the Quality College, he fulfilled two graduate school internships with Philip Crosby Associates, Inc. He has consulted with over one hundred nonprofit organizations, researching and practicing the special applications of quality management in a nonprofit culture, and has provided educational and technical services to dozens more.

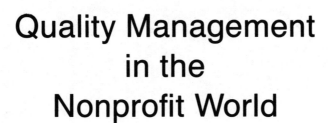

Quality Management
in the
Nonprofit World

The Benefits of Quality Management: Maximum Service and Financial Freedom

A healthy, energetic nonprofit organization that is managing for quality will attract new constituents and reap economic gains.

Benefits to Be Pursued

Each segment of the nonprofit world can obtain its own special benefits through quality management. The individual and corporate values that are produced as you pursue quality will satisfy even the most demanding standards. Nonprofit managers will be delighted to discover that the pursuit of quality will not only improve the services they provide but will also increase the number of people they can serve. Because nonprofit managers must constantly strive to keep their work funded and maintain high service standards, they are enthusiastic when I describe to them how the pursuit of quality in their services also yields the valuable by-products of financial conservation, program marketability, and new and excited contributors.

The clergy composes a very large and significant segment of the nonprofit community. When I speak of clergy, I am including pastoral executives, administrators, staff, and laypersons who regularly confront the difficulties of fulfilling the needs

1

of their constituents with limited resources. They can often experience a sort of "heavenly torment" as they find themselves performing the work of a divine intermediary while grappling with the earthly realities and complexities of their work. The application of quality management principles to their tasks can bring a peaceful order and prosperity which the clergy can especially appreciate. Quality management will enable them to design and organize useful ministries as they are needed and stabilize the management of what is often a fragile economic entity.

Volunteerism is on the increase in our society, and as any manager knows, volunteers can be the lifeblood of a nonprofit organization. Today's volunteers, whether they are board members, trustees, adjunct staff, fund-raisers or workers, want to know two things: how to derive the maximum satisfaction from service, and how to find the nonprofit organization in which their time and talents will be most effective. Understanding the principles of quality management as well as the roots of nonprofit administrative style will help volunteers to evaluate their service opportunities and discover the most effective ways to serve.

Contributors, whether individual or corporate, large or small, constantly face the dilemma of sifting through the solicitations they receive from organizations representing various causes and providing services that are apparently in great demand. The contributor who wants to help a particular segment of our society is often dependent upon an organization that can effectively serve people the contributor may not be able to reach. However, the unknowns of the organization and its performance can create a philanthropic gridlock for the contributor. He or she may be intent on helping and making wise investments but may hesitate because of fears and concerns about the propriety of the gift. Although the risks we take as contributors can never be completely eliminated, understanding the principles of quality management, and the nonprofit world in general, will help. Through the application of these principles, contributors will be able to organize their giving and more effectively evaluate an organization's performance. They may even have an opportunity to provide their favorite cause with some practical management assistance.

Lost and Found Money

Nonprofit managers are always on the lookout for new sources of money, and one of the exciting benefits of quality management is the reduction of operating costs. It is literally money that is being lost or wasted when we do the wrong thing with our time and resources. This found money allows you to do more with the same budget or to build reserves for a time when contributions are low.

Philip Crosby says that for-profit service companies lose approximately 35 percent of their operating budgets in doing things over that were done wrong the first time (1985, p. 2). There is no reason to believe that a nonprofit's percentage should be any lower, and here is what that means. For every $100,000 you receive in contributions, you are spending $35,000 either doing things wrong or doing the wrong things. Let us assume you can serve 2,000 clients per year per hundred thousand dollars. That means you are spending approximately $50.00 per client. If you can recover the 35 percent that is being misused, you could serve 2,000 people for $65,000 at an average cost of $32.50 per person and have $35,000 in surplus for some of the things on your wish list. Another option would be to use the same $100,000 to serve 3,077 people instead of 2,000.

The cost of serving people is spread across your organization from your own salary and time to the cost of typing letters and answering the telephone. Every time someone performs work that does not cause the client's requirement to be met, the costs go up. Each mistake or wasted effort causes the number of people you can help to go down. If you want to serve 3,077 people instead of 2,000, you have two choices: improve quality and raise the same number of contributed dollars, or increase your fund-raising by 53 percent.

I was lecturing to the management staff of a very large drug treatment center when one of the managers put her hands to her face and screamed "Oh, no!" We had been discussing the importance of working with agencies that referred clients to make sure they knew in detail what characteristics made a person referable. She had suddenly realized the answer to a budget problem she was researching and, because of her process knowledge, had calculated that the error could be costing them hundreds of thousands of dollars per year.

The organization had been feeling increased pressure to serve more clients from several agencies that referred people to them. At the same time, they were seeing rapid increases in the average cost to serve a client. Failure rates were up and morale was down. Some critical relationships in the community were in danger because of the performance failures, and pressure was building on the leadership to solve the problem.

Because they had been very successful for many years and were well organized, they had accurate data about what problems they could solve for people and how much time and effort it would require. They also knew what personality and skill variables the client would need to be successful. They had never selected only the most curable people for treatment but there were some minimum standards beyond which failure was certain. In those cases, there were other alternatives that were more appropriate for the client than what the center offered.

Because they had not continued to inform the referring agencies and other community organizations of the rationale for their client standards, new personnel working without benefit of the training were referring people who were certain to fail. Thousands of personnel hours were being lost repeating therapy and solving other problems created by their attempts to help people who were outside the scope of their services. What had started out as a finely tuned and well-managed process had slowly and incrementally become unmanaged. The situation was consuming dollars and destroying the infrastructure of the center. It was also limiting the ability of the organization to meet the needs of those they could help.

Within nearly all nonprofit organizations there are processes that are misusing resources, like the one just described. It is a typical vulnerability among organizations that are trying to do good. On the bright side though, finding and eliminating these errors turns lost dollars into found ones and increases your ability to serve your community.

Successful Fund-Raising

Traditionally, nonprofit organizations have raised their money by appealing to constituents with a good cause. Over the past few years, the systems of development have become more sophisticated, but touching the heartstrings of the contributor has remained a primary thrust. The emphasis is usually on the raw human and emotional aspects of the organization's services. The objective is to cause us to act on the basis of our deep feelings about a particular issue. Typically, they help us remember that we are angry at drunk drivers or that we are afraid someone is going to take away our freedoms. It is also not unusual to have guilt subtly work its way into our consciences. They may try to cause us to feel sorry for another person or ashamed we have not helped, but the desired action is the same — writing a check.

Nonprofit managers are growing weary of the mind games of traditional fund-raising. A person who is managing sophisticated service delivery systems is not as likely to be comfortable kowtowing to the local good old boy or girl network in search of support. The computerized letter and telephone-marketing approaches have left us sour and disappointed as well. The manager dreads using them as much as potential contributors abhor receiving them.

Grantmakers have become frustrated with it all and have counterattacked. While the fund-raising executives meet in one hotel to discuss new word-processing programs to individually stylize each grant package and disguise their production line origin, the grantmakers are meeting in another hotel to review new software to respond to the deluge of grantseekers in ways that "say no without saying it." It is a war of paper. The irony of it is that very little money is given by grantmakers on the basis of good paperwork alone. The big money moves on the basis of relationships.

A group of nonprofit managers interested in providing medical services to the poor asked me to develop a marketing plan to help them through the early years of their development. One of the things they made clear was that they were not willing to participate in traditional fund-raising manipulations. They considered them to be ethically unsavory and beneath the dignity of the service they wanted to provide. They wanted to know if there might be some other more businesslike way to find their supporters. They had done their homework, so when I told them how truly expensive traditional fund-raisers can become when you reduce the actual funds they generate by the costs of salary, expenses, special printing, banquets, and abused constituents, they were quick to concur.

I told them that to be successful they must do two things. First, they would have to concentrate on doing things right through quality management. Second, they would have to use the savings generated through quality management and other funds they could designate to support a key member of their team in building relationships in the community. The person with this responsibility would obviously need to be completely trustworthy and believe in the importance of the mission so much that he or she would be willing to give up hands-on time to make sure that individual contributors and grantmakers knew about and understood the project.

These were professional people who knew how to give and receive tough advice. They chose from among their leaders the person whom they could entrust with their mission's story and then grittily began to make the adjustments I had recommended. In just a few months, I began to receive reports of their success and of special relationships they were forming with major grantmakers. Contributors are intrigued by honest, well-managed nonprofit organizations and they are looking for quality work in which to invest. The fund-raiser with these things to offer will often prevail over the one who is shortsighted.

Goodness and Competence

In fund-raising, as in other areas of nonprofit management, our personal and public attitudes about the goodness of the mission become an issue. The goodness of our mission draws volunteers to our side, and its link to virtue is an undeniable factor in the investment decisions made by contributors. Because it is such a powerful motivation, overemphasis of the goodness of the mission in fund-raising can cause regrettable, but avoidable, calamities.

Touting the goodness of our mission can cause contributors to overlook the errors in our organization. The need for managerial fitness, cost controls, and fund-raising integrity can be rationalized away when the listener is mesmerized by the goodness of the mission. This is especially true when a manager has begun to take the goodness of his or her mission a little too seriously. Staff and contributors alike who are caught up in the goodness of what they are doing tend to ignore the fact that the end does not justify the means.

Goodness must be linked together with personal character, organizational honesty, and competence to have its full positive effect. When it is misused and constituents discover inconsistency, the backlash can be terrifying. Most notable among public examples are the tribulations of televangelists who have violated the public trust of the goodness of their missions. But, lest we pound on them unfairly, there have been other religious and secular nonprofit leaders who have become well known in their local communities for unfairly capitalizing on goodness.

When goodness and competence are not in balance and contributors get close to an organization's service operations, intensely negative reactions can occur. A familiar scenario is that of the well-known local business person who has considered making a grant on the basis of the overwhelming goodness of a particular organization's mission. To further help the organization, the person agrees to allow his or her name to be used in promotional activity. Being prudent, the business person first takes a prearranged tour of the service operations and facilities. He or she might even meet with other contributors at an enthusiastic luncheon or reception before making the final plunge. Everything looks fantastic, and the feeling of goodness is intoxicating.

Amazingly, the business acumen that allowed the person to accumulate the wealth under pursuit is left back at the office. I have heard this story told time and again by disillusioned contributors. Certain things about the day nagged at his or her conscience, apparently signaling the need for a closer look. However, because of the contributor's sincere desire to help and belief that do-gooders work a little differently, the natural urges to probe were resisted. The disheveled business office and awkward moments were rationalized as coincidental. The absence of another well-known previous contributor at the kick-off luncheon was perceived as odd but explainable. So goes the thought processes that in another environment would have provoked further research. The die is cast and the check is written.

The results of poor management and bungled client services eventually become clear as the contributor becomes active as a volunteer and board member. It is at this point in the relationship that many contributors express their feeling of betrayal. I have rarely found nonprofit managers who deliberately conspired to deceive supporters and cover up inadequacies. Surely, we put on a happy face for our visitors, but the real cause of these conflicts is the failure of both fund-raiser and contributor to emphasize equal measures of goodness and competence in their relationship.

Depending on Quality

Very few nonprofit organizations include in their fund-raising presentations anything significant about how they are operating internally or about the errors they have identified that need correcting. That is understandable, because conventional wisdom would dictate that raising money requires an emphasis on all the good things. For-profit companies fill their annual reports with glowing accounts of their products and people, knowing that the public perception of their companies drastically affects stock prices as well as sales. There is, however, one major exception to this conventional approach.

For-profit companies that have committed to quality improvement tell the whole world. Information about their efforts to improve dominate all their communications. They take pride in telling us how many fewer errors they produced this year over last and how happy their employees are now that they are pursuing quality. You must have seen the reports of some of these companies in the media. Inherent in their excitement about how well they are doing is the truth about how poorly they were doing before they began to manage for quality. That fact becomes virtually risk free to the company that is seriously improving its processes. Quality improvement is great for business, and some companies sell their improvement programs more vigorously than their product. The result is higher customer confidence and profit, profit, profit. When nonprofit organizations present their work to potential contributors, customer confidence is the key issue. Doing good and improving services sounds like a winning combination.

In the for-profit market, the person using the product or service is the one paying, whereas the bills of a nonprofit are usually paid by a contributor who will not directly benefit from the service. The nonprofit must satisfy two customers, the client and the contributor, to be successful. There is no question that the difficulty of satisfying two customers in order to obtain one payment for the service provided makes the manager's job more difficult. You know that you want to do the very best job you can in serving your clients, and quality management can make that happen. The only question remaining is how to gain the consistent support of your contributors. When the mission is a good one, you can depend on quality to make the difference.

Human Values and Profitability

Traditionally, the primary measure of the performance of a nonprofit organization has been its effect on the circumstances of its clients. There are many different measures of success with a client, depending on the special requirements and services demanded by the mission statement. However, the time, energy, and money expended to help a client has been considered a profitable investment if the client's needs are satisfied. In recent years though, there has been an increasing emphasis on tracking the cost to serve each client. This has become a measure referred to by both grantmakers and service managers, and it indicates a willingness on the part of the nonprofit world to balance the importance of effectiveness with efficiency.

For-profit managers have traditionally focused on profit with little or no concern for the human values of their work, either for their employees or the communities in which they operate. Now they realize that performance includes their effect on the environment and other social systems as well as the dollars they earn in profits. Even though profit still dominates as the first priority, success in the for-profit arena now balances delicately between the measures of profit and human values. The for-profit manager has learned that the organization he or she leads is most responsive and its goals best accomplished when both of these important motivations are successfully harnessed. On this issue, nonprofit managers generally remain out of balance. The human measures of performance should be the priority in nonprofit work, but not to the continued exclusion of some measures of profitability. In the light of what we have discussed about the effects of quality management, let us look at a few measures that might ultimately be considered as managing toward a profit in a nonprofit organization. For the sake of our discussion, we will define profitability as "measurable increases in human values, security, equity, or dollars available."

For the service administrator, profitability could be defined as managing toward the development of clearly stated and easily performed procedures. The result should be an increase in effectiveness as well as in the number of clients to be served. Every counselor, secretary, truck driver, or volunteer who finds and eliminates a procedural error is managing toward real profitability. This has a positive effect on everyone's job.

To the fund-raiser, it means improved services at a lower cost per client and the ability to compete with other nonprofits for contribution dollars. It also makes research and development money easier to obtain because of the marketability of improvement.

To the accountant, it means conserved dollars through efficiency, increased dollars through marketability, and more credits than debits. It also means long-term financial stability and the reserves to level out contribution highs and lows.

To the attorney of a nonprofit organization, it means managing toward a diminishing liability. Every error that is removed from service processes decreases the risk of loss and increases long-term stability.

To the executive director, it means satisfied clients, good community relations, regular payrolls, and the ability to reward faithfulness and competence in tangible ways.

The Cost of Doing Things Wrong

There are certain requirements that must be fulfilled in order to perform any task properly. Requirements are the "what, how much, when, and how" of the way we do things when they are done right. In quality management, when we have done things right, it is because we have done our work according to specific, agreed-upon requirements. We call it conforming to the requirements. When we do things wrong, it is called nonconformance. Phil Crosby says "quality is measured by the price of nonconformance" (1984, p. 85). It is one of his absolutes of quality management. The price of nonconformance is a calculation of what it costs us when we do things wrong. When we do not conform to the requirements necessary to serve a client right, it can cost dearly in human values *and* dollars. It is in this way that quality and profitability are linked.

If our job is to manufacture a product and we fail to do it according to the correct specifications, it can result in costs to return, repair, rework, replace, or restock the item. In addition, there is the loss of customer confidence and additional purchases, all of which can drastically affect profits. All of these elements run up the cost of placing a product that conforms to requirements in the hands of a customer. The same types of costs apply in the delivery of nonprofit services. When we do things over again that were done wrong one or more times, the additional costs in payroll, administration, and overhead are only the beginning. There are also potential costs in human values for our client, as well as the loss of volunteers and contributors.

Consider the client of a nonprofit organization who receives incorrect counsel, inaccurate direction, incomplete service, or worse yet, a service that in no way meets his or her need. Each time an error is made in the delivery of services, the client incurs a loss. The size of the loss varies with the type of services offered and the possible inconveniences to the client. However, the potential for great losses can be unnerving. When a person who is seriously contemplating suicide calls the local crisis counseling hotline, the counsel he or she receives can dramatically affect not only the caller but family members and friends as well. Likewise, information and referral services that send jobseekers to employers without openings, homeless people to shelters that are closed, or mothers to day-care facilities that are poorly run, may be contributing to the destruction of a client's hope and well-being. It is one thing to replace a dissatisfied customer's poorly manufactured product, but when you are directly affecting the quality of someone's life, you may not get a second opportunity. Even if you do, the costs can be enormous, both to the person who was poorly served and to the organization.

Volunteers and contributors are drawn to a nonprofit because of the opportunity to share in all the good things that are done there for people. They also have their personal agenda for stewarding their time and money. They have a vested interest in the well-being of the clients and the financial efficiency of the organization. When volunteers and contributors are turned off because of indications that things are being done wrong, they have a tendency to jump ship. Besides the loss in volunteer hours and dollars, the organization then suffers from the negative reports of its work that trickle through the community. Each volunteer and contributor has a responsibility to evaluate his or her own requirements for service and determine whether affiliating with a particular nonprofit organization is appropriate. Initially the commitment may have to be made on the basis of the mission statement, but eventually the organization's ability to fulfill its promises and conform to requirements will dominate that person's decision.

The real measure of quality for a nonprofit is how much or how little time and money are spent doing things wrong and how much damage is being done to the clients, volunteers, and contributors. As effectiveness is increased through quality management, the cost of not conforming to the requirements decreases.

The Cost of Doing Things Right

The manager of a successful nonprofit organization helping poor pregnant women asked me to meet with her to discuss the plans for their annual conference. As I entered her office, she was just hanging up from a telephone conversation and shaking her head in disgust. Her frustration was obvious, so I asked what it was about. "You know," she said, "some people don't have enough sense to spend two dollars on a phone call to gain a two-hundred-dollar account." She had been excitedly reporting to an important board member her success in selling out-of-state ads for the conference program and had received a stern lecture regarding cost control.

Her background in marketing and sales had given her confidence to see that there was little or no risk in her sales efforts and tremendous financial potential. The board member was obviously someone trying to administer the organization's efforts without understanding a fundamental principle of enterprise, "the cost of doing business." This creates two kinds of behaviors that are both expensive and counterproductive. One person refuses to spend, gripping quarters so hard they cannot reach out and pick up twenty-dollar bills. The other indiscriminately spends twenty-dollar bills in an all-out effort to find quarters. The manager who is committed to quality management must be willing to spend time and money prudently and provide the leadership to overcome extremist thinking. Quality is not expensive — in fact, as Phil Crosby says, "quality is free" (1979, p. 1). The financial gains from improving quality far exceed the costs. Careful reallocation of your time and energy could quickly supply all you need for your improvement efforts.

The demand for nonprofit services almost always exceeds supply. Because of it, clients either lower their expectations or are replaced by others also in need. Nonprofit organizations can blunder services and do things wrong continuously and still have an abundance of clients. However, it is different with contributors. The typical community offers many nonprofit alternatives to contributors, including some that are performing nearly the same service as your own. The demand for contributed dollars far exceeds those available, so the contributor has little motivation to convince an organization of its need to improve. There are so many other causes asking for support that it is much easier to leave quietly. Quality management is primarily focused on providing error-free services to your client. However, it may dramatically reduce the cost of doing business wrong by positively impressing your contributors.

It is human nature to want to help someone who is trying to improve. Teachers favor students, parents favor children, employers favor employees, and contributors favor organizations that are demonstrating a commitment to improve. The planned and deliberate communication of your improvement process to your community will produce new contributors and bring back lost ones. One of the immeasurable results of doing things wrong is the loss of contributors. Managers who come to the realization that improvement is needed may want to recall some of the negative signals that they had received from contributors and had ignored. The cost of recovering their support may only be a little humility.

Adjusting Your Economic Theory

Economic theory—how we think markets and economies are supposed to work—has everything to do with the plans and strategies we use in management. It is sometimes difficult to convince nonprofit managers that adjustments in their theories are in order until the negative consequences of their decisions begin to accumulate. They are often caught up in the goodness of their mission and express discomfort when a discussion about practical management and profitability arises. They somehow choose to overlook the economic factors that control their car payments, office rental, and a myriad of other fundamentals in their processes. I have a personal theory that this kind of thinking has much to do with the frustration of not having enough money for their mission and a limited ability to obtain it. It is painful to talk about finances and improving process management when our economic theory leaves us without hope of success.

A missionary friend who has traveled the world helping the poor and less fortunate began his work with a theory of provision that quickly proved to be ineffective. He had observed other missionaries in their struggle to raise contributions and was generally uncomfortable with the idea of going from church to church receiving offerings for his work. He believed that there had to be a more practical and less humiliating method to finance his calling.

After much thought, he decided to go out to an isolated orange grove and pray. He had heard stories of great men who had asked God for provisions and received it in a supernatural way outside the natural economy, and he decided to ask for the same favor. He prayed and waited in the orange grove alone all night expecting an angel to appear or money to materialize or something of similar scale. The next day, tired and a little embarrassed, he drove home to report to his wife that he was still penniless.

He had already concluded that he could not save enough from his regular job to fulfill his mission, so he had quit and started a small janitorial business. This business had done well, but he still had found himself considerably short of his goals—thus the night in the orange grove. A little perplexed by his dilemma, he decided to concede the need to ask others for help and continue his business. He told his story honestly to all who asked and soon found that he had been able to accumulate enough cash from his business and the contributions to make his first trip.

You might think it was totally absurd to have gone into the orange grove expecting money to fall from heaven. Whether that is true or not, the important lesson in this story is that my friend was willing to face the facts and adjust his economic theory. I regularly talk to nonprofit managers whose strategies, although not so extreme, are just as impractical. They stiffen at the thought of subjecting their work to measures of profitability. They are either disgusted by the mixture of business and nonprofit service, or fear being perceived as cold and mechanical, or believe incorrectly that they are required by law to manage unprofitably. Because of the interdependent nature of profitability measures and quality management, your success may depend on honest reassessment of your economic values. The wrong economic theory can destroy the viability of your mission.

The Black Hole

The process of decision making carries with it the consequences of any weaknesses in economic theory. For decisions that are dependable, every issue must be thoroughly analyzed using human and profit measures to determine how appropriate a proposed action might be and how capable the organization is of sustaining the decision. Where profitability measures are not adequately considered, the research and planning processes are incomplete and gaps of vulnerabilty are inherent in the decision. When the decision is made and the new service process has begun, the measures used in the decision making are the ones most likely to be used in making evaluations of how things are going. It can be very unnerving when there are no reliable numbers to compare with the human values.

A few years ago, I decided to take flying lessons. I had often been ferried about by other pilots in my work and had many opportunities to "steer" small aircraft, but I had always wanted to fly one. My instructor noted right away that I had exceptional flying instincts. When he would describe situations to me, my natural reaction about what I should do was generally very good. As my "seat of the pants" ability could make the small difference I might need in some situations, it was comforting to know I would have an edge of advantage. The human value of flying is easy to define. It lies in whether or not you can take off, enjoy your flight, and return safely to the ground. However, it does not take very long to figure out that no matter how naturally skilled you are, numbers are very important. Air speed, altitude, angles, and degrees provided by the airplane's instruments are critical.

On a routine takeoff one morning, I suddenly realized that something was wrong. As far as I knew, and these things flash through your mind at times like this, I had prepared for and executed my takeoff roll by the book. Nonetheless, I had a very uneasy feeling jolting through my mind and body telling me something about my flight configuration was wrong. It was clear to me that an important human value, reaching ground safely, was in jeopardy. I can remember vividly how I instantly went over in my mind the steps I had taken, and saying them out loud, I replayed each step over and over in the few seconds I had to determine what was wrong. It was a terrifying experience, not unlike what nonprofit managers must go through when they have made a decision and begun a process primarily on the basis of confidence in their skills and human measures and find themselves instinctively sensing they are out of control. Without reliable information, some adjustments cannot be made and the possible consequences can be intimidating. It is a very helpless feeling.

The cost of doing things wrong can be more than your organization is able to pay. Just on the other side of those irritating little obstacles to your expansion plans is a black hole of consumption capable of draining away your time, energy, and money while simultaneously destroying your contributor relationships and chewing up helpless clients. Many nonprofit managers have experienced the rush of enthusiasm for their plans to build larger facilities, increase their geographical service areas, or add new services to their portfolios only to realize too late that some questions were not sufficiently answered — or more sadly, were never asked. A dependence on goodness or a resistance to practical business principles can create a situation where the most basic planning information is excluded from consideration. In case after case of nonprofit failure that I have observed, that missing information would have been enough to change a trustee's enthusiastic yes vote to a sobering no.

In the following chapters, I will describe three essential operating principles which, when implemented in your nonprofit organization, will allow you to begin to prosper dramatically.

I will also focus on several hindrances I have discovered which, if left unchallenged, will limit your success. Because I was challenged by my instructor to look beyond the joys of flying to the discipline of process management, I am around today to tell this story. I was able to find the solution to my problem (the incorrect positioning of flaps) because I had already committed myself to learn what I needed to be successful.

Chapter Review

Through the application of quality management principles, managers can improve their services and increase the number of people they can serve. The financial benefits include the conservation of misused dollars, program marketability, and new contributors. New services can also be designed and implemented as they are needed. Even volunteers and contributors benefit from a knowledge of quality management. Volunteers can assess their opportunities for service more effectively, and contributors can organize their giving and evaluate an organization's performance before making a contribution.

As much as 35 percent of a nonprofit organization's budget may be lost in doing things over that were done wrong the first time or, worse yet, doing the wrong things. *Multiply your organization's budget by 35 percent.* This could be the number of lost and findable dollars in your budget.

The cost of serving people is spread across an organization and includes salaries, the cost of typing letters, telephone charges, and every aspect of your budget. *Write down your organization's annual budget. Divide that number by the total number of people you now serve.* The result is your current cost to serve a client. *Now multiply your cost per client by 65 percent.* This new number is what your improved cost per client might be. You can either serve the same number of clients for 65 percent of your current budget or increase the number of people you can serve by 53 percent.

Fund-raisers have become frustrated with the pressures of fund-raising, and rightly so. The competition for contributed dollars increases each year. Because so many good things are being done by so many good people, the successful fund-raiser must do two things: first, convince his or her organization to do things right through quality management, and second, take time to build contributor relationships in which an organization's goodness and competence are equally emphasized.

Nonprofit organizations have traditionally focused their measures of performance solely on the client's improvement. However, new ways of measuring efficiency have become commonplace, with the cost per client being one of the first. Profitability in nonprofit work can be defined as "measurable increases in human values, security, equity, or dollars available." When we improve services, increase the number of clients served, conserve operating dollars, and find new contributions, we are operating profitably.

There are certain requirements that must be fulfilled to perform any task properly. Requirements are the "what, how much, when, and how" of the way we do things when they are done right. When we do things right, we have conformed to the requirements. When we do things wrong, we call it nonconformance. Phil Crosby says "quality is measured by the price of nonconformance" (1984, p. 85).

The price of nonconformance is a calculation of what it costs us when we do things wrong. Besides the waste of operating dollars, there can be enormous losses in human values to our clients. We can also lose volunteers and contributors who perceive the inefficiencies or ineffectiveness of an organization. The real measure of quality for a nonprofit organization is how much time and money are spent doing the wrong things or doing things wrong and how much damage is being done to the clients, volunteers, and contributors. As effectiveness is increased through quality management, the cost of not conforming to the requirements decreases.

The cost of doing things right is usually very small in comparison to the price of nonconformance. Careful reallocation of your time and energy could quickly supply all you need for your improvement efforts. Communities and contributors favor organizations that are demonstrating a commitment to improve. The planned and deliberate communication of your improvement processes will produce new contributors and bring back lost ones.

Economic theory — how we think markets and economies are supposed to work — has everything to do with the plans and strategies we use in management. Some nonprofit managers stiffen at the thought of subjecting their work to measures of profitability. They may be disgusted by the mixture of business and nonprofit service, fear being perceived as cold and mechanical, or believe incorrectly that they are required by law to manage unprofitably. Because of the interdependent nature of profitability measures and quality management, your success may depend on honest reassessment of your economic values.

2

Quality Defined: Fulfilling Client, Community, and Contributor Requirements

Personal compassion and practicality are not mutually exclusive in the delivery of services. They are essential counterparts.

Quality Through Process Management

Quality can be deliberately pursued through the application of specific management principles in our endeavors. As you will learn as you progress through this book, it is really the only way to enjoy the quality experience consistently. When you think about it a while, it becomes obvious. The term "quality management" indicates we are managing in such a way as to attain quality in what we do. What we manage are the various processes of our work or mission.

Nonprofit organizations routinely struggle to balance two important processes: (1) the acquisition of operating revenues through fund-raising and other sources, and (2) the continuous expenditure of administrative energy to maintain effectiveness and efficiency in their missions. Many times, the search for financial contributions involves such a great drain of management focus that little is left for the ongoing fulfillment of the mission. In other cases, where an organization doggedly pursues the purposes of its charter and delegates fund-raising to a lower priority, it may operate from day to day worried about its financial solvency.

The argument over which processes are most important and should dominate the manager's attention is very much like the chicken-and-egg riddle. Actually, unless a nonprofit is delivering quality services to its clients, there is little to be excited about when attracting contributors. It is essential that managers focus their energy on the service processes. Ethically, the objective of our service processes is to help people, not to raise money. However, the pressures of financing our work sometimes create a fine line of separation in our motives.

The manager is often in turmoil about the reasons for which he or she was hired — to manage services or to raise money. It can be a major problem for the trustees as well, since the "why" of their hiring process could have been all mixed up in a lot of talk about doing good, while the real concern they had was the financial condition of the organization. Both are legitimate issues. Increasingly, though, more and more managers are being hired on the basis of their ability to raise money rather than their skill at managing service processes. If you do not think so, I suggest you read the display ads in your favorite nonprofit journal.

Service delivery and fund-raising are two processes that are, without question, dependent upon each other, and the success of a nonprofit organization is dependent upon both processes. You may have wondered, as I once did, if there was a system of management that would allow the comfortable integration of these two processes and boost both of them to higher levels of performance. I think you will soon agree that I have found such a system and that you can apply it in your own work.

Mixing Business with Compassion

Most nonprofits provide services that require their staffs to have an understanding of social systems and the specialized disciplines around which their services are centered. A good example would be the element of counseling that is a part of so many nonprofit service structures.

Counseling is a social system with many models and therapeutic approaches, all designed to help someone understand things better and receive helpful information. Trained counselors have learned how to be supportive, when to confront, how to teach, and how to deal with the human psyche. Then they have to learn the specialized information they want to teach. A nonprofit may have more than one social system within its service structure, with counseling topics and specialized therapeutic approaches for each. There must be hundreds of topics, ranging from employment counseling to rape recovery.

The little community center down the street takes on a new complexity when we consider the social disciplines needed to oversee the day-care services, senior citizens activities, drug awareness programs, nutritional classes, and the myriad of other activities most of these organizations provide. Nonprofit managers routinely supervise several highly specialized service systems, and they do it with loving care and personalized compassion. That is a full agenda for most folks, but wait a minute, we want them to be good business people as well.

The task that stretches most nonprofit managers is being effective in both the delivery of services and business management. It is usually this requirement that brings tension into their professional lives. After all, who wants to read a book on management systems or attend a seminar about financial planning when there are hurting people who need your help. A commonly heard complaint after a nonprofit board meeting is "All this discussion about business and money depresses me. I am not in this for money, and I don't like talking about it. I care about people, not all this babble about business. We are a nonprofit organization, not a business."

This person needs to understand that his or her *business* is managing the delivery of services to clients. That includes making sure the bills are paid on time so the services will still be available next month.

If you really care about the individuals you are trying to serve, you must be concerned with making sure all the variables that can limit your ability to help them are under control. That means you must have some specialized knowledge about those business subjects you may think are not a part of your calling. You cannot effectively delegate your responsibilities without knowing enough about them to hold someone accountable for keeping them on track. After all, it is only one more discipline among many you have already conquered.

The principles of quality management will help you to know what information you need, when you need it, where things are going, and where they ought to be. Quality management is focused on meeting the needs of the individual client and improving all that you do.

Goodness Is Not Good Enough

I cannot think of a single person involved in nonprofit work who does not have a story about being drawn to the work because of the goodness or rightness of the mission. Whether they made a decision to sacrifice income and position to serve their community or succeeded in a career early enough in life to want to give something back, it is almost always clear that their motive is to do something good and right for someone else. The wonderful thing is that we live in a society that is structured economically with tax exemptions to promote altruistic work. We are also fortunate that we have prospered so much as a nation that some of us can focus on the special needs among us. There are probably thousands of missions being organized to do good deeds for people with special needs. There are also thousands of managers and staff who have already sacrificed greatly in efforts to serve others, only to fail at their missions.

Many nonprofits fail before they ever receive their letters of determination from the IRS declaring that they are truly doing what they said they were going to do in their applications for tax exemption. They are not unlike for-profit businesses that fail early in their development, many during their first year of operation. That may be surprising to you. You might think there should be a wider discrepancy between the business life span of a company working for profit and another that is doing something because it is good and right. However, most for-profit businesses think they are doing something good and right, too.

Almost no one starts a business without giving thought to the goodness or rightness of what they plan to do, and every organization must produce a product or service that meets a need. The fact that you do not intend to profit personally from the activity does not make you any less likely to fail or succeed. Each organization will bear the consequences of whether or not it delivered on its promises, managed well, and correctly estimated the marketplace's willingness to pay the ticket. What a shock for the person who thinks success rests upon the goodness of the mission! A person in the for-profit world quickly learns that doing a good thing is not enough. There are other people out there doing the same good thing a little better for a little less money who will quickly take away your customers. In the nonprofit world, your competitors will take your clients and your contributors. The fact that you are doing something good and right and trying very hard to help people at great personal sacrifice is, unfortunately, not good enough.

I have met dozens of people carrying a chip on their shoulder who think they failed in their mission because no one understood the goodness and rightness of their work. The real tragedy is that many of them just do not want to believe that their failure had some other fundamental cause. The goodness of what you do certainly adds satisfaction to your work and it can create support from your community, but in the long haul, you must effectively meet needs, manage, and compete with all the others who are doing good things. Goodness is an asset and a liability. It must be kept in perspective as only one of the elements of success. When measuring the quality of your services, the goodness of your mission pales by comparison with the soundness of doing things right.

Performance Is What Counts

When a client arrives at the doors of a nonprofit organization, he or she may be carrying huge personal burdens well beyond the scope of the services offered by the volunteers and staff. It is essential, therefore, that a nonprofit promise only what it can deliver, and that it deliver on its promises. Although every client should expect to be treated with kindness and care by friendly people, ultimately it is performance that counts.

Picture a single parent who is working for minimum wage to support her two children who have been abandoned by their father. Life for this person can be painful beyond description. She faces a constant struggle to provide her family with food, much less fulfill their needs for clothing, medical care, and housing. There are tens of thousands of single parents in our country and, in almost every community, various organizations have sprung up to help these sometimes desperate women and their children. Services include day-care for the children, career and personal counseling, educational classes, housing assistance, and co-ops offering food, clothing, and household items. It is not unusual for these families to receive aid from more than one organization. This increases their opportunity not only for help but also for pain, rejection, and humiliation. Unfortunately, it is often the case that poor organization, training, and preparation to receive clients can create results drastically inconsistent with compassion.

Most people would agree that meeting the needs of the client is the most important consideration in nonprofit work. It is the basis for most of our rhetoric about our mission and the primary performance standard we discuss. In nearly every strategic planning session in which I participate, our focus is on identifying the needs of the client. Those sessions are usually exciting and satisfying because we are developing our dream of helping someone in need. As we talk about specific services and the number of people we might reach with them, we experience one of the most important rewards of our work, "warm fuzzies." The very thought of impacting a less fortunate person's life in a positive way gives us a warm feeling of satisfaction that our time and energy are well spent. The human soul needs to feel good about doing good, and it is a great thing to experience.

Inevitably though, we face the hard work of service. The real difficulty comes when we step back from the process to look closely at what we might do to improve on our work. When we begin to talk about writing down the important steps in our delivery of services and creating policies and procedures to ensure that everyone is doing the same things the same way, we encounter resistance. Discipline, efficiency, and effectiveness through good business practice has a way of sounding cold and mechanical. Not only that, our workers want to be helping people, not writing procedures and creating management systems. The bottom line may be the fear of losing the warm fuzzies. To overcome this fear, people must be taught that compassion for individuals and practicality in business management are not mutually exclusive. I cannot think of anything more personally satisfying and compassionate than knowing that everyone in our organization has worked together to decide what needed to be done, figured out how best to do it, documented the plans and procedures, and disciplined ourselves to do it correctly and consistently, so that we fulfilled our promises to every client.

The Reality of Quality

The quality experiences pursued by nonprofit workers and contributors take place when we effectively and specifically meet people's needs. That is reality. Nothing else counts once you have experienced quality in this way.

I have a good friend who is always exhorting his clients to "be real." I enjoy the way he says it, probably because he makes you feel like it is the right thing to do and fun, too. It is the same way in quality management. No one enjoys the continuous hassles created by unrealistic management solutions and poorly operated service systems. Being real about quality management means taking serious steps to eliminate irritating errors with solutions that get to the root of the issue. Organizations with a sincere concern for the needs of their clients and a committed team of workers can create an environment where people enjoy doing good and doing it right.

Phil Crosby says, "Quality is conforming to requirements" (1984, p. 59). Requirements are nothing more than the descriptions of what needs to be done to do a job right. Without a clear understanding of what the requirements are for our work, we cannot perform effectively, and quality cannot consistently be achieved. Remember, we measure quality by the price of not conforming to the requirements, so we obtain real quality when we conform to the requirements. Our task begins with identifying the requirements for our work. To do this, we must know how and from whom to obtain them.

In the for-profit application of quality management, requirements are obtained from the customers. The customers' requirements consist of what they want from a product or service and how much they are willing to pay for it. The definition of customer includes anyone for whom you are doing work, to whom you are supplying information, and so on. For instance, a secretary's customers would include his or her boss, the people who receive the boss's letters, the people who call on the telephone, and anyone else who depends upon the secretary and/or boss for help, including the final consumer of their product or service. In each case, we must know what the customers' expectations are and what they are willing to pay. How much is the boss willing to pay to get things done the way he or she expects? How much time is the telephone caller willing to spend before the telephone is answered — one ring, two, three, or four before they hang up? Accessibility by telephone in a certain number of rings is a business reality in the for-profit world. A missed call could result in a lost account with a definite price for not conforming to the customers' requirements.

In the nonprofit world, the definition of our customer or client expands even further, because we have to satisfy the requirements not only of our clients but also of the contributor who pays for the service and anyone else in our community who has a reasonable interest in our client. How we conform to the requirements of a local government, hospital, police department, health and welfare agency, chamber of commerce, or service club and their interest in our client has everything to do with the quality of our work and eventually the community's willingness to support us financially. Nonprofit organizations and their clients do not exist in a vacuum outside other influential components of our society. The price of not conforming to essential community requirements can be devastating.

It should be clear by now that goodness is not quality,

even though it is commendable. Sometimes managers misunderstand the message and swing wildly away from an emphasis on goodness and compassion to cold-hearted bureaucratic implementation of services. Remember, we are talking about mixing practical business sense with a client-centered attitude of compassion. Quality occurs when you do the right thing for your clients by fulfilling their requirements. It means using a bandage when it is appropriate and doing major surgery only when it is needed. Supplying a much needed bandage or providing comfort until surgery can be accomplished is a simple service that meets the need and is a pure expression of quality. When we create exhaustive and complex services that are too much or too soon for the need, we are not doing quality work. What should be exhaustive is the process of researching needs, defining them, deciding what services you will provide, and establishing the requirements for how you will do it.

Doing the Mission Statement Right

A mission statement that is clear and specific is the first step in creating quality services for your clients. Nonprofit organizations, contributors, and volunteers sometimes have vague and mystical definitions of purpose. For the organization, this leads to uncertainty about what services should receive priority within its operating structure and ambiguity about its role in the community. For the contributor or volunteer, it can mean a recurring sense of insecurity about what he or she is doing.

Choosing a mission is something that is very often taken for granted. Usually an individual decides to help a particular segment of society either with his or her financial resources or time and skills. In a corporate setting, it can be one key leader who influences the other decision makers to focus on a special need in the community or a certain method of contributing. In either case, the desire for service by one person will often set the initial requirements for the mission. Those requirements may emanate from the person's interest in education and create a focus on scholarship programs. Another individual may start out with a concern about poor, young people and end up with a very similar mission. There are any number of ways to arrive at the same place of service, but almost always it is the result of one person's leadership. Typically, in the development of a nonprofit, that leader will set about finding others who share his or her vision, form a board of trustees, and incorporate. Because the trustees may agree quickly to serve in support of the individual's vision, it may be assumed improperly that the mission being discussed is the right one for this group of people. Before the ink has dried on the new letterhead, the organization could be committed to office space, equipment, and payroll for a mission that it cannot accomplish.

For example, a group of citizens led by an excited visionary might decide to form a nonprofit organization to help the single mothers in their community. It is likely they will spend more time on the choice of a name than on the development of a mission statement that can be fulfilled. As they discuss the number of women they know who are single parents and the various trials they face each day, they may agree surprisingly soon to define their mission as "reaching out to single mothers and their children with practical and compassionate services." That part of their task completed, they would then focus their energy on choosing a name for their organization. At that point, things may slow a little because of individual tastes and preferences about the image the name should project and its marketability. It might even occur to them that choosing a name was harder than anything else they did. They might be shocked to discover that the reason it took so long to agree was because the name was a specific one. Unfortunately, they may find out that the mission statement was much broader than they understood and that it meant many different things to different people. It was not specific enough to bring about the focused debate and discussion that would have slowed down their process.

As mentioned earlier, there are many different missions that can be specified within the broad spectrum of helping single mothers in practical and compassionate ways, any one of which could outstrip the resources and skills of the average nonprofit organization. Often, when I question trustees about a mission statement that I believe is too broad, they will have several viewpoints about what they thought the mission statement meant. As they describe what they thought the organization was going to do, they will invariably focus on that part of the preliminary discussion of the mission statement that attracted them into participation. In the example of the single mothers, it could have been counseling, housing, food, day care, or any number of other specific missions that may have an equally significant number of service structures. The statement of a mission that can be accomplished does not need interpretation. It is clear and specific and it will automatically lead to the next step of organizational development — the selection of specific services to fulfill the mission.

Doing the Client Services Right

To continue our example, suppose the trustees of the new organization had finally agreed on what they believed to be a more doable mission statement — "helping Charleston's single mothers find affordable housing." As we compare this new mission statement with the previous one — "reaching out to single mothers and their children with practical and compassionate services" — we realize there are significant differences in what may be perceived as the services being promised to the client and community.

"Reaching out" has become "helping find." The implications of reaching out include proactive searches in the community for clients. That could cause difficulty later on when the organization tries to obtain money from the city government or other major grantmakers. They will want a description of the outreaches. What contributors might consider to be appropriate outreaches might differ greatly from the organization's intention, which may have been to advertise.

"Charleston" has become the geographic target for the effort. Targeting a specific area can eliminate a great deal of the rejection and confusion experienced by clients outside the sphere of an organization's influence and resources. The previous mission statement had left the service area open-ended. As resources and experience grow, the mission statement can be amended and the service area expanded.

"Single mothers and their children" has become "single mothers." As subtle as this change may appear, when a single parent or someone from the community sees the word "children" in this mission statement, it implies to them "services for children," regardless of what the remainder of the statement says. Like many other nonprofit clients, these women are under extraordinary personal pressures, and consideration has to be given to what they may want to see in the mission statement that is not there.

"Practical and compassionate services" has become "affordable housing." Again, the sky was the limit under the previous statement. The new mission statement speaks to the issue of helping these women find affordable housing. It does not say "providing" because that might imply that the organization has an available source within its own structure.

When a comparison is made of the expectations the client might have had under the two different mission statements, it is easy to see that under the first mission statement, the organization may have been failing to conform to requirements it never intended to fulfill. Nonetheless, the client and the community would be evaluating the organization's performance on the basis of the implied promises. The price of nonconformance would have been enormous. Although this example is not intended to be comprehensive, it does offer some ideas of the self-imposed and publicly perceived service requirements that a single word in a mission statement can represent.

At this point, a list of services that directly support the new mission statement would be outlined. Remember, we are saying "helping find affordable housing," which could be as simple as a referral and information service. In addition, that list of services might include the provision of crisis housing, temporary transitional housing, long-term rentals, home-sharing, benevolence in the form of housing subsidies, rental deposits, and utility deposits, and even help in physically moving furniture and household items. Use your imagination, because both your clients and the community will be using theirs. When the services to be provided are finally selected, it may be appropriate to rewrite the mission statement to eliminate communication gaps.

When we consider the requirements that are received from sources external to a nonprofit, the need for adjusting the portfolio of services and mission statement may become apparent. The organization's research may indicate that it should provide services A, B, and C. However, as interaction with clients and the community takes place, it sometimes becomes necessary to add service D and/or adjust or eliminate one of the other services. Services must remain dynamic within the constraints of the mission statement and the resources available.

Within the organization, the requirements for delivering the services to the client must be established by describing in writing what must be done to do the job right. Policy requirements might include, among others, what information should be acquired in an initial interview with a client and what limits there are on the provision of resources. Procedural requirements would include such details as the what, how much, when, and how — questions that any volunteer or staff member might have about his or her job in serving the client. Those details might include answering the telephone before a certain number of rings and the procedure for finding a replacement when a person's shift is completed, so the telephone is not left unattended. Whatever needs to be known to do the job right must be written down and thoroughly explained to every staff member and volunteer.

Doing the Fund-Raising Right

When the mission statement and client services are defined and agreed to by the leadership, a thorough process of identifying the requirements for fund-raising must be given priority. As mentioned before, the service delivery process and the fund-raising process are interdependent in nature.

The fund-raising manager should have full knowledge of the development process that created the portfolio of services, and when possible he or she should have participated in those decisions. Service managers can sometimes become a little too idealistic in their approach to organizational development and may not fully grasp the processes of fund-raising. When fund-raising managers and service managers work together, they begin to realize the agony and ecstasy of their mutual responsibilities. It brings an honest balance into an organization's management structure. Too often, fund-raising managers are treated like hired guns by their management counterparts. Truthfully, when they lack knowledge of the service processes, that may be what they are. More often, though, fund-raisers are becoming important players on nonprofit management teams. Some organizations have full vice-presidents as resource development officers, and they may be responsible for recruiting volunteers as well. This is a natural division of responsibilities when fund-raising becomes an equal among all the processes in a nonprofit organization.

Fund-raising begins by determining exactly what financial and human resources are needed to accomplish the mission. It is essential for the fund-raiser to understand the personnel requirements because finding an able and qualified volunteer can be the equivalent of thousands of dollars in payroll. The operating budget should also include the estimated costs in telling the organization's story to potential contributors. Once the budget requirements are well defined, an assessment should be made to determine how much of the needed finances and skills are available within the leadership. This is important because when the fund-raising manager begins to assess the community's willingness to support the work, one of the questions he or she will most likely be asked by grantmakers is what or how much is being contributed by trustees. That is a fair question. As they are able, trustees should be the first to contribute.

In the short run, money can be raised on the organization's vision and the promises it makes to help its clients and, therefore, its community. It will not take long, though, for contributors to want to see results. As I have said previously, performance is what counts. The personal contacts, letters, telephone calls, and publications that will always be a part of fund-raising take on a new significance when the story you have to tell is one where you are doing good and doing it right. Each nonprofit has to choose the communication style that will best represent its efforts to the community it serves. Beyond that, the context of the communications must provide clear evidence to constituents that their requirements as contributors are being fulfilled. It is not enough to talk about the results of quality management within the organization. To be truly effective, fund-raising must cause contributors to feel comfortably related to the work by routinely obtaining their requirements through personal contact and publications. When contributors begin to recognize that their requirements have become the organization's requirements, they will experience the reality and the lure of quality.

Applying quality management principles to fund-raising processes is not a quick fix for financial woes. Certainly, contributors will respond favorably to an organization's efforts to improve and they may do so in relatively quick and decisive ways, but the fund-raiser's marketing of quality management has more long-term implications. As a nonprofit organization points to an improvement in its ability to serve its clients, details the specific ways it is establishing and conforming to requirements, and reports its deliberate measurement of the quality of the services, it will be establishing the kind of contributor confidence that is vital to its financial future.

Ask, Listen, Think, Then Do

Managers who want to achieve quality must be capable of restraining themselves and their organizations from acting prematurely without sufficient thought and planning. By carefully identifying requirements and meeting them in an orderly and timely fashion, you will create the market presence needed to succeed. You may also avoid the foolish waste of valuable resources.

To find the best way to do anything right, you have to be ready to ask a lot of questions and listen to as many different answers as possible until you attain a clear picture of what will work. Requirements should represent the specific realities of how a process should operate to function properly. Designing services is no place for guesswork. Sometimes a person's intuition or experience can be more of a hindrance than a help. Certainly, no one should undervalue his or her experience as a tool to evaluate the answers received to research questions, but observations gained from experience are always somewhat subjective. As you listen to a variety of opinions about any given situation, the real value of your experience becomes clearer. If your instincts were right, that is fine. It is the price you pay when you are wrong that should compel you to ask, ask, ask — and listen.

It is essential when researching the requirements for service to listen carefully to what is not being said as much as what is. Never assume that someone has understood the question and has fully answered if he or she says what you want to hear. Researchers sometimes have a tendency to frame questions in such a way that the correct answer is obvious to the respondent. Everyone likes to give the correct or desired answer. It is funny sometimes how a person responding to a research question may assume from the way it is presented that the researcher already knows the answer. To avoid hearing only what you want to hear, it is good procedure to repeat both the question and the answer as you heard it. Thank the respondent and then ask if there is any other answer he or she can think of that might be helpful. Always obtain clarification if there is any doubt about the completeness of an answer, especially when it is something you did not expect or want to hear. Never assume. Work at getting to the truth as the respondent sees it.

I have observed a tendency among some nonprofit researchers to avoid asking people with veto power questions concerning the organization or development of their intended services. For instance, it may be that a person developing services for a drug rehabilitation center may try to avoid complete exposure of his or her plans to someone in a state or federal bureaucracy, even though he or she will eventually be serving clients who may have to receive the bureaucracy's approval in some way. Finding resistance early in the development process is much better than encountering it after significant time and resources have been used to develop a service that may not be acceptable to someone whose requirements may differ. Instead of ducking the issue, uncover the points of resistance and use that additional input as a way of fine-tuning the operating requirements. You can convert opposition to support very easily in the early stages of development by adding someone's special requirements to your design. Later on, changes can become costly and result in negative public perceptions. Sometimes people will wonder, and rightly so, how a project got so far along before its leaders discovered the error of their ways.

It is fairly common for the draft mission statement to be broad and somewhat vague. As the leaders take time to think over their research information and evaluate the accumulated service requirements, the resulting mission statement and service design may become relatively simple. The time invested in carefully researching and planning the work is likely to be far less than the price of nonconformance for services that are incorrectly conceived.

The Open Book

When I perform on-site evaluations for grantmakers or consult with nonprofit managers, I have a routine that helps me gain insight into what makes the organization tick. I like to tour the facility to get the feel of the overall environment, as well as review items like the mission statement and portfolio of services. Although most organizations have brochures and descriptions of their services, fewer have policy and procedures manuals, and even fewer have outlined internal processes and described them in written form.

The requirements that link the mission statement, the description of services, and the delivery of services are what I want to know. For instance, what are the community's requirements that would cause this organization to be needed? Which of them guided the development of the mission statement? What were the specific client requirements that shaped the portfolio of services? Which organizational and client requirements defined the staff job descriptions, and so on? If this information was not written down, the history and philosophy for what now exists is usually hidden in the minds and experiences of the leadership, staff, and volunteers.

It is impossible to measure performance or to hold ourselves accountable without some record of specific requirements. Guiding an organization without them is like touring in a foreign country without a map. A lot of time is spent backtracking and asking for directions. The task for me as a consultant is how to critique what is happening or offer strategic planning insights without a record of established requirements. Finding the requirements is simple; it is like reading an open book. Where there are no written requirements or in those situations that are not open to your close investigation, you can still identify the requirements that are guiding the efforts of the organization. You may not have considered it, but we live and act in conformance with what we really believe is important. What we believe is important may have no connection at all to what we say is important, so do not be convinced by rhetoric alone.

You may say that you are concerned about the poor people who live down the street from your house. You know you are supposed to help them and may be vocal about it to your family. However, if you are not helping those poor people, it is because you do not believe as strongly that you should help them as you believe something else that is limiting your ability to help or otherwise causing you to behave in a manner inconsistent with your words. We all do what we believe the most. Organizations do what they believe even though what they say may sound a little different. Those things that we believe the most become the requirements that cause our behavior. If I want to know what the unwritten requirements are for an organization, I observe what they are actually doing and work backward to what requirements those behaviors could represent.

For example, when you observe what happens in some churches in America, you can quickly deduce that there has been some agreement that their two primary requirements are to provide a comfortable setting, stimulating religious speeches, and entertainment for their parishioners. When you listen for the words that confirm these priorities, they are usually centered around the need to retreat from the pressures of life and be refreshed before returning to the daily routines. Some other important requirements might be to train the parishioners for serving one another and the community. This would be manifested by an organized educational thrust with classroom instruction and practical training. Still other requirements may be to provide mercy for the homeless, orphans, and widows. When these expressions of religion are agreed to as important, the human and financial resources are organized and released with great zeal.

You can identify the importance of the requirements by the amount of time, energy, and money attributed to each activity. Their priority is evidenced by the percentage attributed to each. In this respect, all organizations work the same. Whether we have a written guide to faith and moral behavior like the Bible or whether we have just agreed to these things informally, what we really believe, we are doing. The requirements that guide our actions are an open book for all to see.

Chapter Review

The acquisition of revenues through fund-raising and the delivery of services are two important processes that are dependent upon each other and upon which the success of an organization depends. An organization that is providing quality services will find fund-raising to be easier. A sufficient flow of finances from contributions is critical to the delivery of quality services.

A successful nonprofit manager must be able to manage service delivery and business processes with equal discipline. The principles of quality management help the manager know what information is needed, when he or she needs it, where the processes are going, and where they ought to be. Quality management is focused on meeting the needs of the client and improving all organizational processes.

Almost everyone involved in nonprofit work believes in the goodness of their mission, and many people make personal sacrifices to serve in the nonprofit world and help people. However, goodness is an asset that must be kept in perspective; it is only one of the elements of success in nonprofit work. When measuring the quality of your services, the goodness of your mission pales in comparison with the soundness of doing things right. All in all, everyone is doing something good. Performance is what counts.

Poor organization, training, and preparation for receiving clients can create results drastically inconsistent with the compassionate intents of service. Although discipline, efficiency, and effectiveness through good business practice have a way of sounding cold and mechanical, compassion for individuals and practicality in business management are not mutually exclusive. They are essential counterparts.

Quality management is a way to take serious steps to eliminate errors in client services and improve finances. Phil Crosby says, "Quality is conforming to requirements" (1984, p. 59). As was said before, requirements are the "what, how much, when, and how" of the way we do things when they are done right. We can find out the right things to do and the right ways to do them by asking our clients, our communities, and our contributors what is important to them. *Who are the clients in your nonprofit setting?* You may be serving more than one clientele. *List each of them and several of each one's requirements.*

A mission statement that is clear and specific is the first step in creating quality services for your clients. Sometimes mission statements are too broad in their scope, which makes the selection of services more difficult. A clearly written mission statement represents specific needs in your community and will be easily understood by clients, contributors, or other members of the community you serve. *List the services that your organization's mission statement specifically states or implies.*

Every client service should be compared to the mission statement and the specific needs of clients. A single word can dramatically change the community's perception of the mission statement and what services are available. When the services to be provided are finally selected, it may be appropriate to rewrite the mission statement to ensure that it reflects the chosen services. *List all the specific services your organization is providing and then write down what client and community requirements each one fulfills. Compare this information to the services implied or stated in the mission statement.* They should be consistent with one another.

The internal policies and procedures of an organization should state how each service is to be structured and what is expected of each person in the process of delivering the services. What you actually do should represent specific client and community requirements. *Are your organization's policies and procedures written and accessible to those who need to know them?*

Personal contacts, letters, telephone calls, and publications will always be a significant part of fund-raising. It is helpful when the story you have to tell is one where you are doing good and doing it right. It is not enough, though, to talk about the results of quality management within an organization. You must make contributors feel comfortably related to your work by routinely obtaining their requirements. When contributors begin to recognize that their requirements have become the organization's requirements, they will experience the reality and the lure of quality.

To achieve quality, you must ask, listen, think, and then do. Obtaining client, community, and contributor requirements and then fulfilling them is the path to success. All organizations are the same. What we really believe, we are doing.

3

The System of Quality: Finding and Eliminating the Causes of Problems

Whether we are helping people or improving service processes, we must work to prevent the reoccurrence of problems.

Doing Good and Preventing Bad

There are so many people who need help with problems that are too big for them to solve alone that the opportunity for someone who wants to do something good for others is almost limitless. Helping people overcome life's obstacles and improve their conditions can be an enriching and deeply satisfying experience. When staff and volunteers first enter the nonprofit world in service to their community, they are usually preoccupied with the work at hand and plunge deeply into the routines of service. It does not take long, though, before the repetition of clearing away the rubble in people's lives begins to trouble them. At some point, it may occur to them that they are only dealing with the "effects" of problems, and they begin to wonder if there might be some way to prevent the problems from occurring in the first place. There are some very definite ways in which the nonprofit world answers that question.

Some organizations believe that the particular problems with which they are working are so large or complex that they cannot really be solved. This does not cause them to give up and stop doing good. To the contrary, they focus only on doing good. There is something to be said for sincere acts of mercy toward people who may be beyond changes that will bring them back into the mainstream of life. Without doubt, there are clients who have been so devastated by life that the right thing for a worker to do is to provide loving and kind support, while meeting their human needs. In many cases, it is appropriate to expect the client to acquire some life skills, with the worker's help, that will prevent the problems from recurring. It is obviously important that some wisdom be used in deciding which clients can or cannot contribute to the improvement process. A woman eighty-five years of age, with heart disease and living alone on a social security check, needs mercy and comfort. Her participation in improvement and prevention efforts may be minimal, and rightly so. On the other hand, a twenty-five-year-old spouse abuser might reasonably be expected to adjust his or her attitude and behaviors so that the marital relationship does not continue to produce violence. Where prevention is a reasonable expectation, it has become a norm in nonprofit work.

In some cases, prevention strategies include helping the client recover from the effect of his or her problem, working with the client to prevent a personal recurrence, and then going beyond that to make certain that the problem does not continue into the next generation. A good example of this approach to service would be the assistance of the urban poor. Short-term help may be provided to a client in the form of food, clothing, shelter, medical care, or other necessities. At the same time, education, job training, and other personal services may be provided to help the client prevent some of the causes of poverty. To prevent the continuance of poverty into the next generation, the client's children may attend special day-care programs while the client receives instruction in parenting. There are a number of philosophies and approaches to prevention in service, and over the years I have heard them discussed in groups working with teenage pregnancy, drug dependency, alcoholism, crime, and so on. Prevention has become a common element in the client services of many nonprofit organizations.

In this chapter, I will take the concept of prevention into the internal processes of an organization and apply it to the elimination of errors in the delivery of services.

Common Prevention Methods

When I think of the commonly held notion of prevention, I remember a television commercial that shows a woman preventing her party guests from doing damage to the carpet with food and drink by making incredible diving catches and darting from one potential disaster to another. This is the typical understanding of prevention — working faster and harder and pressing the limits of endurance to outrun, outdistance, and outmaneuver errors. It is a pretty frustrating, and exhausting, way to live. The television commercial recommends a specially treated carpet that resists stains. That would prevent permanent stains, but it will not prevent the need to clean up the carpet after a spill. At the Quality College, they prevent spills by putting lids on the coffee cups. No spills, no stains, no cleaning, and only a little bit of inconvenience. That is real prevention.

Another approach to prevention is the "nag and prod" method. This is actually a form of avoidance rather than prevention, and is practiced most by parents. It requires that you constantly monitor the movement of your little flock and caution them about the perils and potential errors of their actions just before they are ready to act. The reason this method is most noticeable in parents may be that they are so concerned that their children do things right. Nonprofit managers are usually somewhere in the same category and are very susceptible to this style of management. This continuous state of alert requires energy, intensity, and a lightning-fast mind. It is probably one of the most difficult behaviors for managers to maintain and results in an oppressive environment that sooner or later will lead to a revolt. When workers begin to look away and avoid your attention or begin to give single-syllable answers to your questions, it is a good indication that they do not want to endure another lecture on how to do it right.

The "try harder" method of management is a problem throughout industry, not just in the nonprofit world. A classic example is the nondelegating manager. He or she needs to be a part of every committee and group, all processes, and every decision, so that he or she can prevent bad decisions, impractical processes, runaway groups, and all the crazy things committees come up with. This is especially true when people have been unfaithful to us in the past. Sometimes experience teaches us that no one else cares about the client as we do, so it is necessary to press hard and stay involved in all the processes.

The mechanism that causes us to continue inappropriate prevention styles is simple. What we are doing to prevent errors only has to work one time and we are hooked. Psychologists tell us the most powerful form of reinforcement is the variable and unpredictable schedule of satisfaction. Catching one piece of cake before it hits the floor, intercepting one error with a brilliant display of perception, or discovering one committee that would have gone the wrong way had it been left alone, is all it takes. Anyone looking objectively at the examples I have mentioned will be able to see that if you try these methods hard enough and consistently, you are going to prevent some errors. Each time you succeed, you may become less reasonable and more possessed by your sense of self-justification. You tell me: How much would you enjoy the party if the hostess were poised at your feet ready to "prevent" your inevitable spill?

Assessment, Appraisal, Assurance

Modern quality methods have their roots in aerospace engineering. I grew up in an aerospace environment. My father worked on several important military projects at Cape Kennedy and was deeply involved in the management of quality. I was familiar with the language of quality even as a young boy. All my relatives and neighbors worked in aerospace, and it was routine for them to sit around the kitchen table talking about the pressure on them to do quality work. Deviations, tolerances, samples, and other such terms were all part of our daily vocabulary. I even understood the codes and abbreviations.

When I heard Dad talk about "buying off a D.R.," I knew he was talking about approving the repairs or corrections that had been completed as a result of a written discrepancy report.

A discrepancy was something that had been done differently than the way it was designed or prescribed. Workers lived in terror of having their work "tagged with a D.R." I realized that all of this pressure to do things right was because of the importance of the work that was being done. We were racing Russia for dominance in outer space and maybe the future of our country. I could not wait to take my place in the pressure cooker.

My first real job in the space program was as a data systems analyst on the Apollo Spacecraft Program. We called ourselves "data grunts" because what we did was so tediously repetitive. Each day various tests were run on the spacecraft systems. The tests were conducted according to carefully scripted and rigidly followed test procedures. Engineering data were collected on special strip-chart recorders that looked something like very large electrocardiograph machines that you might see in your doctor's office. There were other specialized recorders that documented every switch that was turned on or off and what happened. A quality control inspector sat in front of each recorder checking off the events as they were performed and annotating the strip charts with a marker. Engineers and test conductors further documented the scripted events and watched over every detail with scrupulous accuracy.

The pressure for mistake-free work was so great that I can remember breaking out in a cold sweat just walking into the control room during a test. It was like being on the bridge of a Star Trek spaceship, but I rarely relaxed enough to enjoy it. I was there for one reason. I took pages from the sacred script in the quality engineer's book, walked a few paces down the hall to photocopy them, and then replaced the pages, always receiving a look of annoyance from the owner of the book. With all those checks, rechecks, and double checks, my job was to check once again to make sure that the notes made on the script matched the ones made on the recorded charts and to write a discrepancy report on any differences. Then we carefully rechecked the data on the charts to see if someone might have missed some event or variance that deviated from procedure.

Mine was one of dozens of such quality control procedures created to raise the level of the "assurance of success."

There were "reliability" engineers who used special statistical methods to predict how many times something might fail in a million repetitions. They routinely took samples of things that did not even look sampleable. Everywhere, assessments and appraisals were in progress to find and correct any errors that might have been made. The truth is, all that effort did not produce quality. All it did was give us a report. The real value of the information lay in how we could use it to change our scripts and improve our processes. When we found ways to change the way we did things so that our processes worked better, we improved quality. The rest of the time we were just finding errors.

In the for-profit and nonprofit sectors of business, the primary emphasis in the pursuit of quality continues to be finding errors that have been made. For nonprofit workers the options are very clear. We can count all the people we hurt and bury those numbers under the warm fuzzies of the ones we have helped, or we can use the same information to cause us to pursue improved processes and services. Usually, the information we need is close at hand. The outcome of its use depends on our attitude toward the facts and our faith in improvement.

Unmanaged Processes

When you look closely at the processes in some nonprofit organizations, you may find that they are not being managed in a deliberate way. The process may be producing a desired result most of the time, but may occasionally veer suddenly off course. Instead of pursuing the causes of errors in a service process, managers are sometimes content to force the process back on course, thinking that their time might be better spent in other areas of responsibility. When internal processes have not been given sufficient attention and the causes of errors identified and removed, there may be a serious potential for paying a catastrophic price of nonconformance.

When I was newly married, my wife marveled at how quickly my mother could whip up a meal in her big iron skillet. We could be sitting around the living room, watching a football game, and just mention food, and in what seemed like only moments, be savoring the aroma of hamburgers, home fries, and coleslaw on the side. Mom had a grip on this simple process that was mind-boggling. In fact, it was not a miraculous feat at all in her mind but a routine display of homemaking. One day my wife, Dorothy, and I were sitting at the kichen table when she noticed a disfigurement of the cabinets near the stove. Taking a closer look, she saw that a vinyl liner that shielded the cabinets had been melted and had attached itself to the wall. She had discovered another part of Mom's reputation. When I was a child, it was a common occurrence to be playing in the backyard and suddenly hear the kitchen door burst open and see my father racing out with a flaming iron skillet in one hand yelling at us to clear the way. He had become just as skilled at getting that skillet outside into the Florida sand as Mom was at setting it on fire. This is the classic example of the unmanaged process.

There is absolutely no question about the product Mom was able to produce when it made it to the table, which it did most of the time. The problem was that we never knew when we might unexpectedly be diverted into a fire drill and a trip to the local take-out chicken place for dinner. To be honest, I enjoyed all the excitement and the chicken, too, but Dad did not share my enthusiasm. He was only too aware of the catastrophic possibilities of this recurring error in Mom's cooking process. The fact that it was not being consistently managed was clear, and as far as he was concerned, it could use some adjustments.

If you sit in the backyard of most nonprofit organizations, it will not be long before someone comes blasting through the backdoor with something that looks like a flaming skillet. Then the battle begins. The firefighters will probably ask if the wonderful service they are performing is really worth all the trouble and risk or if it is time to shut it down. The service providers will point out how the service is badly needed and well received in the community. On one side of the argument are the service providers protecting their right to process, and on the other is the firefighter who is ready to end it all. In virtually every case where there is this kind of struggle, there is no written procedure that outlines the process — what happens at each step along the way and what the final outcome should look like. When the service providers and firefighters sit down and write these things out, what takes place is an arbitrator's view of success. Usually the firefighter begins to see that, with some specific adjustments in the process, the errors can be eliminated and the risks minimized. When the service providers take a closer look and loosen their defenses, they can help find ways to eliminate the errors and improve the service their clients receive.

The process that is documented, agreed upon, and thoroughly conformed to becomes the delight of all parties involved. Everybody wins. The organization becomes stronger and the client is well served. Sometimes processes can be secured and preserved with a minimum of change. In my mother's case, it was a matter of not letting the telephone distract her from a hot skillet. When hard analysis shows us we are off target and need process changes, it is time for decisive leadership. Getting your organization to focus on the dangers of unmanaged processes and create change will be one of your most difficult management challenges.

Prevention in Process Management

When nonprofit organizations establish specific operating requirements for their services, they experience an immediate increase in quality. The simple process of writing down what a client needs and how to go about providing it brings what they are doing closer to what they should be doing. The next step in obtaining quality improvement is to provide regular training for every staff member and volunteer, making sure they understand the principles of quality and the specific requirements of the service process in which they work. Again, the quality of services should improve because when everyone knows the right things to do, there will be fewer errors in the delivery of services. Before long, though, it may become clear that with all that has been done, there are still recurring errors in client services. The way to eliminate them is through the application of the next operating principle of quality management.

To raise our performance levels and consistently achieve quality, we must systematically and thoroughly manage every service process to prevent mistakes from occurring. One of Phil Crosby's absolutes in quality management is that "the system of quality is prevention" (1984, p. 66). In this context, it means that we should focus some of our organizational energy on the continuous reexamination of our general operating requirements and the processes we have established to fulfill them. The objective of prevention in service processes is to go beyond the correction of mistakes that are made and cause the service processes to produce conforming services instead of nonconforming ones. We prevent clients from receiving the wrong services by finding out what they really need and establishing appropriate services. We prevent staff and volunteers from doing things wrong by showing them how to do it right through written procedures and training. To prevent mistakes in client services after these steps have been taken, we must routinely compare established client requirements to current ones and audit our written procedures and training. As client needs change, so do requirements. What was the right thing to do last month may not be so today. We may also find errors in the way we have described the right thing to do to our staff and volunteers, who may be providing nonconforming services because they are doing things exactly as they were trained. Experience may also tell us that our procedures and training were incomplete, overlooking areas that were essential to consistency in services.

The staff of an organization operating a free medical clinic found that they had opened their doors for service one morning without the supplies they needed. The lack of syringes, antibiotics, and vitamin packs would severely alter the quality of their services. To correct the error, they needed only to send someone to bring the forgotten items to the clinic. To prevent the situation from occurring again, they wrote out a checklist of supplies needed to operate properly each day. Then they established a procedure that gave someone the responsibility to compare the checklist to existing supplies frequently enough to prevent running short. That person also made sure that the correct supplies were available in the examining rooms when the patients arrived each day.

Prevention is not always so obvious. What needs to be done to correct and prevent a problem may take more comprehensive evaluation and action. One of the free clinic's doctors began to notice that clients were not returning for follow-up visits which they were asked to make. A thorough review of procedures showed that the clients were receiving reminder slips as they left and even follow-up telephone calls to confirm their appointments. The doctor was puzzled about the cause of the problem and how to prevent it from continuing. Follow-up interviews with a few of the clients who failed to return provided the information he needed. A volunteer receptionist had been dispensing free advice and counsel to the patients while they were waiting for medical care. She was untrained and apparently unaware of the embarrassment and humiliation she was causing the clients as they waited. The clients were unwilling to return for treatment and endure the receptionist's well-intended but unwanted invasion of their privacy. The receptionist's job requirements had to be rewritten and training procedures reworked to prevent the recurrence of the problem.

Establishing a prevention mentality within an organization is really quite simple. Every time a mistake is found, we should obviously do what we can to fix or correct the error. We should also think about what can be done within our service processes to prevent that error from recurring. Sometimes an error represents a simple human failure. These are impossible to eliminate and should be graciously acknowledged. However, when the same mistakes and problems continue to recur, our first thoughts should be about prevention.

Focusing on Cause

I have done a lot of troubleshooting in my work as a consultant. Nonprofit managers regularly describe some occurrence in their organization or services which is troublesome and ask for advice about how to resolve it. What I usually give them is a short-term fix and a process strategy for eliminating the cause. Sometimes the problem is not systemic and requires only a minor fix in a relatively isolated process. Even so, unless I can track down the cause of the error and eliminate other possible contributing factors, my advice is not helpful.

When people describe a problem, they usually describe the effect — reports being late, employee turnover, something or someone not working the way we expected. To improve processes and services, we must track down and document causes. The simplest way to find the cause of a problem is to talk to people involved in the process and ask them questions. There are no better sources of information about the causes of drug addiction than addicts themselves. There is no one more qualified to describe the causes of poor office communications than the people suffering because of it. They can lead us to the cause with amazing accuracy. Unfortunately, when people think of cause they have a tendency to think of *who* rather than what. Because of the fear of being blamed for errors, it is common for people to point frantically in another direction or clam up altogether. It is going to be important to eliminate blame from your culture if you want to isolate causes regularly and consistently. When you are head-hunting, the jungle can be amazingly silent. If it is understood that you are no threat, it can become very noisy.

I remember a situation in which I was called in to evaluate the appropriateness of an organization's mission statement and how well their services reflected their purposes. Coming from the "outside," I have a preset agenda I want to accomplish in my interviews to establish rapport and confidentiality. Included in that is my philosophy for researching management and services. It is simple and direct. I already know who to blame — the people at the top. They are the ones responsible for the policies and procedures and the ones with authority to make changes. What I do is give the staff and volunteers a risk-free opportunity to tell it like it is. I collect some garbage, of course, but for the most part I find valuable historical records.

In this particular case, the young woman I was interviewing said that a key employee had stopped by and told her not to tell the consultant anything. "They will not listen to him if he does tell them, and why take the risk?" She was only partly correct. Someone near the top of her organization had such a fear of being blamed that he had deftly suppressed the flow of information. The senior managers were completely unaware of this and routinely noted that they were receiving no negative feedback.

The solution was simple. I encouraged the senior managers to begin to establish contacts throughout the organization for informal discussion and exchange. Without undermining the established authority, an atmosphere of collegiality could be established where everyone was treated as a partner in the endeavor. When given the opportunity to speak fearlessly, most people will happily share responsibility — and that is exactly what happened.

A Communications Process

When I was in elementary school, the principal regularly made announcements about how important it was to attend class every day and do our very best. She also mentioned that somewhere out there was a truant officer, lurking in the shadows to catch any of us who had decided to fish or play hopscotch when we were supposed to be in school. Things were a lot simpler then. As a nation, we had a much more tender conscience about what we did, and this simple little communications event was enough stimulus to help us along in doing the right things.

Life has become so complicated that today simple truancy has given way to delinquency and drug addiction. If you look at the mission statement and portfolio of services of a community center just twenty years ago and compare it to a recent one, the differences will astound you. Communications and educational initiatives have become dramatically more complex and sophisticated because the problems and the people are different. As nonprofit managers, it is easy to see how our clients' needs have grown and changed. It is equally important to recognize how different our staff members and volunteers have become.

Simple obedience is a thing of the past in human resources management. People today expect to know why things are done the way they are. They also want to be part of the decision-making process and to experience open communication with management. Actually, they should know what they are buying into, especially in a nonprofit organization. Staff members will be asked to make sacrifices almost daily that require a clear understanding of "why" in order to maintain commitment. Volunteers have too many options from which to choose for service to be expected to follow leadership blindly. It is not only everyone's right to say and know, it is the right thing to do as a nonprofit manager.

The importance of staff communications as a process in the management of our mission and the delivery of services cannot be overemphasized. Effective staff communication is a continuing process that changes and grows to meet the challenge. It must provide opportunities for education and change so that the way we think and behave continues to serve the changing needs of our organization and clients. In quality management, this is generally referred to as cultural change, since it may go against the established ways we already think and act. Short-term training and orientation programs that are closed-ended are not sufficient to meet the communication challenges of managing in today's nonprofit environment. Things are changing too rapidly and the pressures are becoming greater by the hour. Communicating with everyone in our organization and keeping them up to date is a major task that requires deliberate planning and an established process of interaction.

When we learn about new ways to do things, a continuing communications process will provide a routine opportunity to share our experiences with our coworkers and take responsibility for the errors of the past. Communication must be honest and open. When staff communication is considered a priority process among all others, it will test the reality of every worker, and provide an information link that is vital to improvement.

Living Healthy

People and organizations that have a healthy lifestyle take responsibility for finding and eliminating the causes of their problems. A healthy organization is a fun place to work. The services it provides consistently meet the needs of its clients and, because of that, everyone enjoys a good reputation in the community. That good reputation translates to a broad constituency base and financial support. The staff enjoys its work, and good working relationships are the priority. This sounds great — and it can be accomplished with less time, energy, and resources than most nonprofit organizations are probably already spending.

I know people who have tried program after program in an unsuccessful effort to become healthy and lose weight. They really want to lose weight, some for beauty, some for health alone, and others so they can have extra energy. Each attempt brings some weight loss, but before long they have regained their old weight and then some. It is really sad to see good people try and fail repeatedly and never obtain lasting results. The problem with nearly all of these programs is that they do nothing to change the fundamental processes of life in order to obtain weight loss and health. They do not deal with causes but are designed primarily to alter the effect. Programs come and go; processes continue.

Let us apply this thinking to your organization. To be effective, management systems must focus on uncovering the causes of problems and preventing them from happening. Your analysis must be comprehensive and continuous. Finding causes and preventing errors must be as much a part of your business practices as opening the front door each day. Prevention must be in place every day, all day, in every area of your work. It is a whole new way of thinking.

Management programs are no different from weight loss programs. There are all kinds of seminars, methods, and philosophies about how to do things. Some of them will work for you and others will not. Quality management helps you decide which method or system is really needed. The way to do that is to be involved constantly in evaluating requirements, finding the cause of problems, and establishing corporate lifestyles that are healthy and real. If you look into your file cabinet or on your bookshelf, you will likely find some evidence of "gadget management" with which you either tried and failed or which you evaluated and rejected. Like the overweight person who, after years of frustration finally rejects shortcuts, it may be time to say "enough is enough."

Choosing Bandages or Surgery

Nonprofit managers must daily face difficult decisions about where to put their time and energy. Like everyone, we have limited resources with which to accomplish the day's miracles. More than once, I have discussed the principles of quality management with an eager leader who must decide how to divide his or her organizational time between improvement and survival. That might sound foolish, since improvement is many times the only way to survive, but there are often harsh realities we must face. A person who is not sure his or her organization has the finances to continue, much less improve, must have some other options from which to choose.

Nonprofit managers are believers. They actually think they can make a difference and they usually do, so finding the motivation for improvement is not a problem. They can see how quality improvement can help their clients, their staff, and finances. What they need is a realistic and practical way to get from where they are to where they want to be. Fortunately, quality management is not high-browed intellectualism but down-to-earth common sense.

When we begin to look at our organization with an eye to preventing errors, it does not take long for some obvious problems to stand out that need fixing. If I find an error in a volunteer training manual, I know right away that the manual needs to be corrected and replaced. The fact that the manual now has my attention may cause me to see other things about the training process that are either outdated or do not meet my current requirements very well. It is not unthinkable that I might see the need for a completely new training system as a result of having discovered just one error in a training manual.

The quality improvement process is very likely to uncover problems that are more widespread than you had first perceived, and that is good. What is bad is when the need for major changes and the time and expense associated with it paralyzes you into inaction. Do not be afraid, ashamed, or embarrassed by the need to apply a bandage where it will help until surgery is a reasonable option. Fixing is only wrong when something more is needed and a quick fix is all you ever plan to do.

A friend of mine recently told me about how she needed to be helped along in her plans for some upcoming surgery. The way she tells it is very comical. It seems that during a routine checkup her doctor found she had a serious need for surgery. Her immediate reaction was that she did not have time to put her career on hold and take nearly six weeks out of her schedule. As she waited and pondered her decision, she found to her amazement that another physical problem she had tolerated would require surgery as well. It was much less serious but, if done by itself, would require another four weeks away from work.

Her doctor was becoming agitated with her resistance, but he knew that it was going to take creative leadership to get her into the hospital. The doctor, who was her friend as well, had known for some time that she was toying with the idea of some cosmetic surgery that would take only a few days away from work. On her next visit, he outlined a proposal that would accomplish all three of the surgical goals during the same six weeks needed for only the first. With some simple planning and prioritizing, the recovery times could be overlapped. My friend became excited about getting started, knowing that she would gain both physically and emotionally. The resources required, which seemed enormous when considered separately, appeared to be very reasonable when restructured into a process. Getting what we really want out of a process can cause the plans we make for improvement much easier to accept.

The Prevention Trap

Finding and eliminating the causes of errors can become a daily adventure. However, like many concepts in life and management, prevention can become a two-edged sword. Although it is an absolute necessity in providing quality services to clients, when left unrestrained outside the limits of manageable processes, it can become a destructive force.

The single problem of drug addiction in America involves millions of people, with so many facets to each person's problem that no single group focused on one aspect can bring permanent change to the overall situation. For example, our federal, state, and local governments have law enforcement people pursuing both the buyer and seller, trying to punish them for their behaviors. They also support dozens of social services aimed at everything from methadone support systems to urban job training projects and almost anything conceivable that could fill the continuum of social concern. Private sector initiatives have created thousands of 501(c)(3) organizations that attack on various fronts. Public foundations and community-based grass-roots groups are raising social awareness and public sentiment. Public education is fighting for order in the classrooms and hallways with projects designed for motivational changes. Religious groups are involved at every level of need with an almost limitless number of variations for solving the practical and spiritual aspects of addiction and personal care. All these groups and many more are attacking the problem of drug addiction with their own measure of zeal, dedication, and sacrificial commitment.

There is so much demand for drug treatment services that the thought of preventing drug addiction in our society is almost unfathomable. It is not that we lack debate about prevention, but that we have difficulty agreeing on what initiative or group of initiatives would prevent a huge problem like drug addiction. Some people believe that supply-side prevention is the appropriate solution. The range of suggested initiatives includes everything from the bombing of Colombian drug factories to instant execution of drug dealers. They might be good ideas actually, but we cannot reach agreement on them. Then there are the thousands of demand-side initiatives, from "just say no" to urban renewal projects. Beyond agreement on philosophies of prevention, we would need strategic plans and resources to execute our agreed-upon initiatives. Almost no one really believes these things will happen. The prevention of drug addiction in America appears to be beyond reach.

To be effective, prevention initiatives must be within the limits of our influence and resources. Whether we are operating as an individual or as a well-organized nonprofit agency, there are going to be limits to our ability to prevent problems outside of our individual or corporate authority. For prevention to take place in an individual's life, that person must give you authority to help him or her. It is impossible to dominate clients and make them prevent their problems from recurring. The same principle applies to communities. Prevention requires the willing cooperation of the individuals involved to be successful. Even when you obtain the authority you need to initiate prevention services, the cost of doing things right could be more than the individual or community is willing to pay. In regard to America's drug problem, the will to cooperate is sometimes offset by a greater concern, such as the right to privacy. Because we place such a high value on the right to privacy, the use of drug testing has very limited effectiveness in preventing the price of nonconformance in our society. The price we have to pay to prevent problems sometimes costs us philosophically and financially. In any case, both authority and resources must be committed. Trying to initiate prevention beyond an organization's ability could create a black hole experience that will consume its resources and destroy its vision.

Prevention should begin inside the organization. If the leadership can discipline themselves to focus on internal processes and prevent errors in the delivery of services from reaching their clients, they will have accomplished much. Services that help clients prevent recurrence of their problems, and provide skills that they can pass on to the next generation, continue the prevention mentality into our communities. When a nonprofit organization understands the limits of its influence and resources and chooses a mission of reasonable size and scope, it can sustain the quality experience — doing good and preventing bad.

Chapter Review

Helping people overcome life's obstacles and improve their conditions can be an enriching and deeply satisfying experience.

However, it may occur to the nonprofit worker that the work he or she does only deals with the "effects" of problems. More often, today's nonprofit organization designs services to meet the immediate need and prevent its recurrence. *List some of the ways your organization's services prevent the continuance of your client's problems.*

The concept of prevention can be applied to an organization's service processes so that our clients do not receive inconsistent services. When we try to do better and think about preventing problems, there are some commonly held notions and methods. They include working faster and harder and outrunning, outdistancing, and outmaneuvering errors; the nag and prod method, and other ways to avoid problems and try harder. Although they sometimes work, they do nothing to eliminate the causes of problems. *Describe a way that your organization has tried harder without preventing problems.*

Some companies try to inspect and assess their products so that defects do not reach their customer. In a service organization, this is more difficult, if not impossible. In either case it is a very time-consuming — and thus expensive — effort that does nothing to eliminate the causes of problems. When we count errors and compare them to satisfied customers, we only have our scorecard. That same information can be used to pursue the improvement of service processes and eliminate errors. *Describe some scorecard information your organization documents that could be used to improve processes.*

An unmanaged process is one that normally produces the desired output but occasionally bursts into flames, leading to debate about its value. Usually when the process is outlined and documented, the causes of the errors can be identified, and the services can be conserved and improved. Getting an organization to focus on the dangers of unmanaged processes may be difficult until there is a crisis caused by one. *Think about your organization's service processes and write down the situations that will inevitably create a crisis.*

The simple process of writing down what a client needs and how to go about providing it should improve the quality of your services. As each staff member and volunteer is fully trained and understands the processes, quality should continue to improve. Sometimes, though, we continue to experience recurring errors in our services. When this happens, we must reexamine our operating requirements for each process and make sure our design is correct. We may be doing things wrong because we are doing exactly what we were trained to do. Phil Crosby says that "the system of quality is prevention" (1984, p. 66). In this context it means that we should focus some of our energy on the continuous reexamination of our requirements and processes to eliminate the causes of errors.

When we pursue the causes of errors there is a tendency for people to think about who rather than what. Because of the fear of being blamed for errors, people often either clam up and say nothing or point in another direction for cause. Blaming must be eliminated from an organization in order to obtain the process knowledge needed to eliminate the causes of errors. When the leadership is willing to honestly take the blame for all errors, it is surprising how often people will speak up and share the responsibility. *Can you think of situations where you were trying to solve a problem in your organization and encountered blaming?*

People today expect to know why things are done the way they are. They also want to be part of the decision-making process and to experience open communication in the workplace. A continuous process of communication and education provides opportunities to share our experiences and take responsibility for the errors of the past. Staff communications that are honest, open, and a priority will provide the information link that is vital to improvement. *Think of ways you can convert your routine staff meetings into continuous processes for improvement.*

People and organizations that have healthy lifestyles take responsibility to find and eliminate the causes of errors. A healthy organization is a fun place to work, and the services it provides consistently meet the needs of its clients. The organization enjoys a good reputation in the community, and that reputation translates into financial support. Problems may seem enormous when added up individually. But when they are integrated into a process of improvement, the benefits become even larger. *Make a list of some of the recurring problems in your organization and describe the price of nonconformance for each one.*

4

Setting Standards for Quality: Achieving the Priorities of Compassion and Performance

The essence of compassion is clear thinking and the practical management of reality.

Resetting Our Standards

The pursuit of quality will provide significant opportunities to reevaluate our individual and corporate standards. The simple accumulation of requirements for client services will cause us to compare the "what, how much, when, and how" of what we are doing with the reality of our clients' needs. When we discover that we have been fulfilling requirements and doing quality work, our reaction to the concepts of quality improvement will be positive. It is when we discover that something we have been doing with the best of intentions is actually not meeting a client's requirements, or that our theories for service are questionable, that we may encounter difficulty. Resetting our standards will test the honesty and maturity of every person in an organization.

Quality improvement will require changes in thinking and behavior in our individual and organizational lifestyles. As any counselor might tell you, the path to behavioral change goes directly through the important constructs of what we believe.

The tender spots in our attitudes about our missions, the services we provide, and our previous experiences with change, will inevitably become the target of reevaluation. When we consider new ideas or reconsider our own ideas with a new openness, the possibility of achieving improvement is dramatically greater. In my own experience, I have been surprised when concepts I thought I could not or would not surrender were eventually proven to be the most significant limiters of my success. Of course, the more good experiences I have had in changing how I think about things, the friendlier change has become.

The dilemma most people encounter in setting new standards for service is in deciding whether they should give up the standards that already exist. When a mentor is not present in our lives or we lack sufficient structural accountability, the willpower needed to assess our basic thinking and attitudes is enormous. It is much easier to lapse into established patterns of thinking, especially if we have become even slightly successful in our work. A small amount of affirmation squeezed from successes can go a long way toward insulating our consciences from conviction about needed changes. The nonprofit manager who is committed to improving quality will have to place a high priority on the deliberate probing of the depths of his or her motivations, management style, and philosophies of service.

The Place for Motivation

When I was primarily involved in the pursuit of profit, I had the opportunity to participate in several motivational schools as a student and teacher. We learned motivational techniques from some of the better-known teachers and then taught them in our own business regions. As mentioned before, I was raised in an environment of quality consciousness and began my adult career deep in an engineering culture, so the hype of motivational technique was a little foreign to me. I had been exhorted to try harder, work longer hours, and do better as an aerospace worker, but what I was then learning as a for-profit entrepreneur was something quite different.

I was representing a major financial services institution with a reputation for integrity and service. Because they were so spotless, it never entered my mind to question the validity of the motivational training I was receiving. However, my wife sensed right away that something was wrong because of the new look in my eyes and the attitude I began to display about business and life in general. I had become compelling and demanding of myself and others. It would be many years before I would understand why.

Motivational techniques commonly used in business settings are designed to cause people to overcome their inner resistance to certain behaviors. These techniques usually do not enable a person to lose his or her fear or the cause for resistance, but they provide an intensity of purpose and energy necessary to overcome them. Most salespeople hate the insecurity and rejection associated with direct sales and, in nearly every case, that does not change. What is offered through motivational techniques is a positive stimulus strong enough to overcome the fear of rejection so that the desired behavior can be performed.

For example, a salesperson might be a mousy, weak personality at home and a less-than-imposing figure on the job under normal circumstances. In preparation for a sales interview, the person could sing a special song of victory, talk about success to himself, or dream about a new home or car. The sales interview becomes the hurdle to fulfillment, and all of the person's energy is released to attack the obstacle with zeal, precision, and a confidence that masks inner fears.

Actors use these techniques to find their character's intensity or to stay in character for long periods of time. It is not surprising that actors depend on this course of motivation so heavily, because that is exactly why we all use it — to get into character, to act. These techniques have been successfully adapted to many areas in the public and private sectors. The sense of mission we have in the nonprofit world causes motivational techniques to be even more powerful.

The problem with motivational techniques is that you are the same mousy person during your performance as you are at home; you are just acting differently. No real internal change has taken place. In fact, the only changes are a further sense of insecurity and personality disintegration. Gains in productivity that are obtained through superficial motivational techniques or promotional campaigns are no substitute for a rational approach to management that changes our way of thinking.

The destructive capability of motivational techniques has been well demonstrated in all areas of business endeavor. Their end result is the consumption of the inner person for external gain. When motivational techniques are applied organizationally, the human resource toll can be enormous. In the short run, things appear to be improving, but before long the organization loses its abiility to continue the external behaviors. It must then face the reality that its energy would have been better used in establishing realistic requirements and fulfilling them.

Quality management will create enthusiasm naturally that no motivational techniques can sustain. The place for personal motivation is in the practical application of principles that cause lasting change.

The Whys and Hows

There are two questions that any nonprofit worker should consider, whether he or she is a volunteer, a staff member, or a manager. They strike at the heart of our motivation and business philosophy. "Why do I do my work the way I do it?" "How can I do it better?" Asking ourselves those two questions and answering them honestly can provide the information we need for analysis of the practicality and reality of our philosophies of service. This is particularly important for those who establish policies and procedures at the staff or management levels, because the whys definitely affect the hows.

There is one answer to the why-question that can be troublesome in creating personal and organizational momentum toward improvement. It is more than likely unknown and hidden in a complex system of ideas, events, and attitudes that could easily disguise the depth of our personal needs. In and of itself, it is not a fatal flaw but, coupled with the how-question, it can render a devastating blow to quality improvement. The response

I am describing is, "I do my work the way I do it because I need to be needed and to be perceived as a good person." On the surface, this seems harmless enough because nearly everyone shares the commonality of those desires. However, the intensity of the need for acceptance, and the effect it can have on a nonprofit worker's ability to think clearly and make objective decisions about *how* to do things, is critical.

Not all things done in the name of mercy or compassion are necessarily so. Some are the result of a person's need for acceptance or of a personal bias that influences the ability to provide rational leadership. It is possible to convince yourself and others about the appropriateness of your management style while allowing a misguided sense of compassion and caring to drain mercy away from the place of greatest need. When this happens, the client may receive a shallow and empty demonstration of social awareness instead of real compassion.

Consider the possibility of a manager, dominated by his or her personal needs for acceptance, who must decide who will be served by a nonprofit organization. There are almost always more clients than there are resources. This could easily place the manager in the uncomfortable position of saying no to someone in need. He or she might find it is much easier to say that the organization will try to serve everyone who asks — but is that necessarily serving with compassion?

Let us assume for our discussion that it takes four units of compassion to help the average client attain healthy self-sufficiency. Let us also assume that the manager can produce a total of forty units of compassion from his or her own life each week. This person can provide four units of compassion for each of ten people. Beyond that there is a point of diminishing returns where the manager must withhold some compassion from those he or she is already helping in order to be compassionate to an additional client. Soon, as the client load grows, fewer and fewer clients are receiving enough compassion to become really healthy. The process stagnates and the quality of the service decreases because the manger's personal needs for acceptance cause him or her to try to serve too many people.

A common solution is quickly to add another worker to

take the extra load of people wanting help. The new worker may only have personal capacity for thirty units of compassion and his or her training and experience may not meet the requirements. But, because of the premises under which the decision is made, we might say that he or she is "better than no one." Again the service level deteriorates. The manager's poor judgment causes the process to become even more unmanageable until we have no idea who is getting what and why.

This scenario is played out daily in nonprofit organizations that have not understood that the essence of compassion is clear thinking and the practical management of reality. It is better to do an effective job for a few than to do a poor job and create false hope and disappointment for many. The stewardship of human resources is a heartbreaking and agonizing experience for the nonprofit leader. This is no place for a person who is unclear about why and how he or she is serving.

Clear and Practical Thinking

At one time or another, nearly everyone has heard the exhortation to work smarter, not harder. Most people would agree that the implication that we can work less physically and more mentally is appealing. I do not remember when I first heard this little gem, but I can recall times when it came as a rebuke for not thinking before I acted, creating more work for myself in the process. Since those times, I have begun to notice an unfortunate change in the public's understanding of the meaning of this phrase.

Until recent years, working smart meant finding a better way to do things. More recently though, working smart has become for some a synonym for finding a way to spend less time and effort for more money. The commonly held ethical and moral limits of only a couple of decades ago no longer constrain some of us in the delivery of our services. This is particularly demonstrated in the absence of prudence in some current business philosophies. The dictionary tells us that a prudent person is "judicious and wisely cautious in practical affairs." When we consider the "junk bond" financed leveraged buyout (LBO), we can see how thinking has changed. Before the modern LBO, leveraging meant borrowing some money for your purchase and securing the loan with real assets. Then it became common for the purchase price to be obtained by borrowing 90 percent or more from institutions willing to take risks considered insane only a few years ago. The borrower is thereby released to dismantle the purchased corporation and sell off its parts in a race against time and compound interest. Financial gains are obtained through the destruction of healthy processes of productivity.

Unfortunately, this high-risk, charging-down-the-hill mentality has also found its place in nonprofit management. It is an "end justifies the means" type of leadership where superficial activity is emphasized over process. We apparently believe that if we act like the Wall Street guys we can have big successes too. In most of these cases, any activity that promotes the nonprofit organization is considered good, and rational feedback from a managed process is virtually nonexistent. When a flashy, hired-gun, fund-raiser who knows little or nothing about service processes is hired to boost an organization's public image and contributions, the immediate excitement may overshadow the price to be paid in human values — and eventually dollars.

Whether or not we are thinking clearly and accepting or rejecting new ideas has a lot to do with how much struggle is taking place in our minds between new principles and previously held ones. For some it would be easy to avoid the Wall Street mentality because of an anti-materialistic viewpoint. However, as many of the hippie generation have learned, anti-materialism can be just as far out of balance. More than once I have consulted with people who have struggled with routine business discipline and self-organization only to find that previously held attitudes about material management have been thwarting their progress.

One particularly clear example is that of a close friend with whom I had counseled in the nonprofit and for-profit sectors for several years. He is an extraordinarily talented individual whose business acumen has regularly been the target of criticism. He had been called unorganized, forgetful, and other unflattering things that were attributed to the artistic and sensitive nature of both his skills and personality. We all know someone in the nonprofit world whose ineptitudes are overlooked or excused as unsolvable. My friend had also gained this unhappy reputation. Each time he lost his keys, forgot an appointment, missed a deadline, showed poor judgment, or otherwise demonstrated a lack of organization, it was attributed to his mellow personality or flower-child background. For the most part, my friend accepted this assessment as a reasonable explanation of his behaviors, although something within him battled the label.

We talked for hours about how to organize work schedules and manage work processes, only to find that his ability to retain the lesson in daily discipline was nearly nonexistent. The breakthrough came when he shared with me one day an anti-materialistic regime he had followed while studying with a certain mystical teacher. He had deliberately told himself not to be concerned with time, material objects, and many of the things essential to being personally organized in business. Prior to that time, he had been a materially successful person. Afterward . . . well you know the story. In this case, the solution was simple. He rejected the guru's way of thinking and gave himself permission to be materially responsible. He began to astound all of us with his entrepreneurial discipline. For the first time in almost twenty years, he could think clearly about practical things.

The principles of quality management may come into conflict with our previously held ideas about nonprofit service. In each case, we will need to reflect on the conflict and, through personal introspection and adjustment, come to a place of clear thinking.

The Threat of Perfection

The next section in this chapter is about a concept in quality management known as "zero defects." Before I explain what it means, it is important for you to know that it does not mean perfection.

Nothing in this world is really perfect. No diamond is completely flawless. No two pieces of metal are exactly the same, and gold is never really 100 percent pure. If you are married, that means the ring on your finger is not perfect. The wedding ceremony probably was not perfect either. No marriage is perfect, not because of the rings and ceremony, but because of the two people in the partnership. Notwithstanding all these imperfections, the rings, the ceremony, and your spouse met the desired requirements at the time.

Although nothing or no one is perfect, sometimes things so fully meet our requirements that we say they are. Our new car fits our personality "perfectly," or the blue suit looks "perfect" on us. These are words we use to say that certain things have met our requirements extremely well, not that they are flawless.

We call someone a perfectionist who works harder than all the rest of us or who is never satisfied with the way something is done. The perfectionist does not appear to be as happy as we like to be or as peaceful, so striving for perfection does not appeal to most people. In fact, when we talk about doing better and eliminating errors, the thought that we might be talking about perfection can create some very negative reactions. The threat of such expectations can be paralyzing, preventing us from functioning normally and thereby creating even more mistakes in our work. The reactions we see against perfection are not without cause.

Nonprofit work has historically found its roots in religion. The motives and ethics of helping others in need and providing mercy or comfort to those less fortunate have always been associated with religion. It is very common for individuals involved in nonprofit work to express privately the religious basis for what they do even if the mission or service they provide is not of a religious nature. I mention this as a prelude to what I believe is an important cause of anxiety in relation to improvement.

The thought of taking an employee or volunteer who is untrained or unskilled in performing a particular service, placing that person in a system of processes that are unmanaged, equipping him or her with faulty tools, and then expecting perfect work, sounds pretty merciless. Yet, in many religious and nonprofit circles, this is very similar to the harsh concept of life and management that people expect to endure. People who have progressed through life with these expectations have accumulated a sizable reservoir of fear and resentment. They react sharply to any thought of being prodded into what they may wrongly anticipate to be a heartless and guilt-producing system of improvement with unreachable goals. I am happy to report that the system of quality I am proposing is not so unreasonable. It presupposes that no one is perfect, and that perfection cannot be attained.

The pressures of quality improvement are comparable to those you might experience taking an open-book test with a helpful tutor at your side. First, the tutor teaches you what you need to know according to the tasks you will need to perform and the questions you will be asked. Then sufficient time is given for review and study. With the book open and the questions before you, the tutor helps you find the answers and supports you through the process. The expectations are reasonable and doable because the resources, processes, and support are in place.

Zero Defects and You

I played a lot of baseball when I was a kid. I was an outfielder who depended heavily on quick reactions and good judgment rather than blazing speed. I did not have the running ability of most outfielders but played an above-average game by paying attention to details, a strategy I learned from my father.

For instance, by knowing our pitcher's style and watching the batter's swing and foot positioning, I could determine that certain portions of the field were less likely to be landing spots for a hit ball. By concentrating on the pitched ball as it approached home plate, I could anticipate the trajectory of a ball hit toward the outfield and react so quickly that it might have seemed I was moving before the ball was hit. This approach lowered the risk of failure so significantly that I was able to outperform others who were more naturally endowed with athletic ability.

The concentration required to perform well became second nature after hundreds of repetitions. I could stay relaxed and enjoy the game while contributing to its outcome. Occasionally, I could even make an outstanding play, stretching the limits of my ability and usually surprising myself, even though I was performing on the basis of established fundamentals. Improbable plays were systematically being eliminated from my improbable list as I made them. Following good basic procedure was reshaping my limits of probability.

The concept of zero defects stretches the limits of some people's understanding of probability, but because it is not perfection, it is completely doable. It is based on a commitment to fulfill the client's requirements every time. A defective service is one that does not conform to my client's requirements. If my client is my boss, zero defects means not sending out a letter with errors in it. If my client is my mother, it means putting the correct number of plates and forks on the table every night. If my client is a soup kitchen patron, it means having clean tables and plates and good food every time we serve. Zero defects is the performance standard established for a process by any person who wants to do things right every time and not present a client with a service that is defective or imcomplete in any way. Phil Crosby says that having zero defects as your standard for quality is an absolute in management (1984, p. 74). Over the next few pages, my goal is to convey the practicality of a zero defects standard.

I was taking questions from the audience at a New England university following a lecture about quality when one of the participants asked the ultimate zero defects question. The woman who posed the question was the administrator of a nonprofit medical institution helping newborn babies in physiological crisis. The babies who were treated in this unit were extremely sick or otherwise gripped by a life-threatening circumstance from birth. She described the incredible commitment of her coworkers and the heart-rending decisions they made day after day and literally minute by minute, trying to save the lives of the little children in their care. She expressed tearfully that it was already their desire to meet the requirements every time, yet nothing they could do would prevent the death of some of those babies. How could quality improvement and zero defects help their situation?

First, I explained to her that unless we could obtain godlike abilities, there are certain impossibilities in life. However, I suspected that knowing they could not save every baby did not ease their pain much because they were always wondering what they might have done better. As the parent of a little boy who died in crisis the first week after birth, I had some understanding of her trauma. It was a unit just like hers that struggled to save the life of our son. I knew very well that supportive and encouraging comments are not enough when unanswered questions gnaw at your guts. With that preparation, I told her about zero defects. Although they could not be perfect and save every baby, it was possible for her and her coworkers to be committed to meeting each baby's individual needs and to manage their resources so well and the processes so carefully that they could be fully confident that no known method or procedure was left untried and that nothing they did contributed to the loss of any baby. The look of relief and hope on her face said it all. You can apply the story to your own circumstances and bring your organization to a defect-free commitment.

Strategies and Statistics

Goal-setting theorists have all sorts of ideas about everything from how to improve our position in the marketplace to increasing the size of our checking accounts. Like some weight reduction plans, they can produce some short-term results.

Some theorists think you should believe you are twelve feet tall and can outrun a bullet so that you can excel as an outfielder. That might improve things a little, but sooner or later reality will settle in and you will feel a bit foolish and tired.

Others will say that you should believe that you have godlike authority and that, as a medical worker, you can save every baby very time. The kinds of unreality this can produce are not easily untangled once they begin. What starts out as simple meditation can end up in a confusing maze of metaphysical hype.

Still other theorists will say that you should measure your greatest possible reach for improvement and then double it, knowing in advance that you will fail to meet the greater goal but will surpass the lesser.

Since these techniques, and many others, are primarily motivational, it is no wonder they fail miserably when applied to the real problems of improving quality. We have already discussed the importance of accumulating client requirements, managing processes, prevention, and thinking, clearly. It is not surprising that reasonable and rational people trying to improve their work might look for something more logical than improvement slogans. On the surface, zero defects sounds unreasonable to some people. Actually, without the hard work and cultural changes we have discussed, it is very unreasonable. The elimination of errors takes time and effort, but it is attainable.

One moderate approach to achieving quality through goal-setting theory is to establish reasonable increments of improvement. A reachable target is chosen and once the goal is reached another goal is established and so on, until the ultimate goal is reached. This means that if you are currently failing fifteen times in one hundred attempts to serve your client properly, you might set goals of reducing your errors to ten and then five and ultimately to zero. Human nature being what it is, this approach has some serious problems. If people know the goal is ten errors per hundred, they are more likely to overlook some of the ten they know they are committing. The fallacy here is that we are not good counters when we are counting our own failures and trying to stay within the prescribed limit. When we think we have committed only ten errors per hundred, we could be at twenty or thirty and honestly not realize it.

Another more common method is to set an acceptable level of quality and live with it. A goal of only two errors per hundred would appear on the surface to be quite a lofty target for some organizations. Let us assume that the processes that bring the service to the client have a moderate number of individual steps or functions, such as twenty. If the person at each step is operating on the premise that two failures are allowed in one hundred attempts, the statistical probability is very discouraging. A reasonable prediction of the total number of errors in a twenty-step process that is targeting a 98 percent success rate is found by taking $.98 \times .98 \times .98$ twenty times. The result is about an 80 percent success rate or twenty failures in one hundred instead of two. If you think that is bad, think about the poor folks who are trying to count errors and stay within ten per one hundred.

The only way to improve consistenty is for every person at every step in each process to try to prevent every error from reaching the client. Quality improvement will not come overnight. It will come in increments and it will be maintainable as long as you never treat an error rate as acceptable. It is reasonable to expect that people will make mistakes and that improvement will come gradually. It is just as reasonable for zero defects to be your standard for quality.

Establishing Supplier Standards

The best restaurants in the world have one very important common attribute. The senior chef personally buys all the food. When you consider that a chef is, in fact, a culinary chemist, it makes sense that the only way a consistent taste can be achieved is with food that meets specific standards. What a chef is able to place on the table before you is completely dependent upon what the suppliers have made available for the chef's use. Style, ambiance, and artful presentation count for nothing if the food does not meet the taste test. Because of the critical nature of consistent supplies, it is a priority to the chef to build a strong working relationship with each wholesaler. The exact nature of the chef's requirements are clearly described, and the wholesaler maintains a good relationship by partnering with the chef and refusing to deviate from the established standards.

In the nonprofit world, the effect that suppliers have on the delivery of services is sometimes overlooked, if not completely ignored. Other priorities dominate our agendas, but none is more able to sidetrack results than supplier failure. Whether supplies are purchased or received as contributions, they should meet specific requirements before they are paid for or receipted. Without supplier standards that are closely regulated, you will find yourself becoming the dumping ground for all kinds of substandard and unusable resources. This is particularly true of donated supplies and services. The best policy is that substandard gifts are no gift at all. They create extra work and poor morale, and they can drastically affect the delivery of services.

My wife and I have been heavily involved in collecting, sorting, and distributing clothes for the less fortunate in our community. We learned early in our work the importance of helping our clients maintain a sense of dignity and not serving them in a way that created a sense of shame. We had convinced our church to designate for our purposes a small building they owned, and we made sure that it was painted and spotless. We had the latest in clothing racks donated by a local retailer and everything was bright, colorful, and uplifting. Our clerks were trained to treat people as though they were paying for their services.

Our suppliers were members of our church and others from the community who had heard about our "store" and wanted to contribute clothes. The standards for clothing were clearly established and adhered to by each contributor and volunteer. We were not a trash receptacle for junk clothes, but a place for clothing to continue to find good use. We refused to accept clothing that did not meet our standards. Junk that was left on our doorstep found its way to the dumpster or was sold to make rags. We gained a reputaiton for quality, and above-standard suppliers beat a path to our door. What a pleasure it was to know we were doing good and doing it right.

Purchased supplies are no less important. Nonprofit managers sometime approach suppliers with an attitude designed to get better deals or outright contributions. It works because of the power of manipulation but it costs the manager in lost support and self-image. It is also more likely that he or she will receive substandard supplies and service. If I have no money, I do not shop in ways that let everyone know it. I tell them what I need and explain my standards. I also explain that I am shopping ahead of time and will come back later to make my purchase. People who want to reduce their price or contribute outright prefer to do it on their own initiative.

It is the same for professional services such as those normally provided by accountants or attorneys. The need for holding all our suppliers accountable to reasonable standards is never more apparent than when a grantor asks for routine paperwork to complete our grant and we cannot deliver because our supplier did not deliver. Products and services that are substandard are not worth the price even if they are free.

Establishing Volunteer Standards

Volunteers are among the most important suppliers that nonprofit managers depend on to continue their work. They supply valuable human resources which, when properly engaged, can be worth tens of thousands of dollars in conserved personnel costs to even the smallest organizations. On the other hand, volunteers who are shoddily introduced into an organization's processes or who are not well managed can create chaotic inconsistency in services. The additional time, energy, and money needed to clean up well-intentioned but off-target volunteer efforts can quickly offset any gains provided by their services.

Managers cause most of the problems with volunteers by making unreasonable assumptions about their intentions and capabilities. My experience has shown that a good or bad volunteer situation is primarily dependent upon the organization's preparation to work with volunteers and the processes that are in place to manage them. I remember one client who had decided that volunteers were much more trouble than they were worth, only to discover that his greatest accomplishments were dependent on loyal and well-trained volunteers. He had complained that volunteers would spend literally thousands of dollars for airline tickets, hotel accommodations, food, and car rentals to participate in an outreach, but would not spend time or money to prepare for their missions. He did not understand that people who were that motivated to help were expecting him to show them how.

I have been volunteering since I was a teenager. I have done everything from helping little old ladies cross the street to highly sensitive personal counseling. I have also been a volunteer organizer and trainer for organizations great and small. Without question, the volunteer experiences I have had as a follower and as a leader that provided the most personal satisfaction were those in which the volunteers understood clearly what was expected of them. A job description and list of duties for each volunteer can eliminate most of the negative potentials for the manager. It will show the volunteers what they are being asked to do and will also help the manager see what type of volunteer is needed for each job.

Volunteers should be recruited and interviewed systematically the same way you would recruit paid staff. An orderly and professional approach to volunteer management will pay off handsomely for your organization. What you do in the recruitment phase of your work will set the standard for volunteer performance. If you are disciplined and well organized, you will often attract more qualified volunteers.

I like to obtain commitment to a specific responsibility and for a given length of time whenever possible. It is also critical to both give and receive a commitment to complete a course of education and training. All volunteers should be instructed to understand fully the requirements that the organization is designed to fulfill. It is the manager's duty to see that the volunteer knows what it means to do things right and how to do them.

Volunteers should be held accountable just as though they were being paid top dollar to work. This does not mean that you can be careless about people's feelings. Even for-profit managers have learned that managing and supervising requires certain social graces and sensitivity to every individual. However, the reluctance of nonprofit managers to hold volunteers accountable to reasonable levels of performance or to terminate bad volunteer relationships can be their downfall.

Because I like to use an organized approach to volunteerism, I have not had many bad experiences with volunteers. I have found, however, that people sometimes volunteer for the wrong personal reasons. It is the unusual volunteer who will participate in recruiting interviews, classroom instruction, and personalized training from supervisors and not expose his or her ineligibility. The key is to know how many hoops you should require volunteers to jump through before you turn them loose in your organization or with your clients. Too many and you can lose good volunteers, but you have probably lost your best volunteers by imposing too few requirements.

The volunteers who are the most valuable are those who have done what it takes to be prepared. Those who complain about the time it takes to prepare will almost always fail to perform well. I decided a long time ago that I would rather face those issues up front by establishing requirements and procedures for new volunteers and allowing the process to do its work.

The People Fixers

My wife and I travel together on business quite often and we compare insights and observations when we have visited a new client for the first time. We have had the pleasure of seeing a lot of wonderful work being done by some incredibly talented people. If you were to sit in the back seat of our rental car or next to us on the airplane, you would most likely hear us talking about some of the especially gifted or unusually loving personalities we had met during the day.

One day, after just such a visit, my wife turned to me and said something that only an experienced visitor would know about the nonprofit world. "It is really amazing," she said. "There are so many different human problems to be solved and so many variables in each situation, but everywhere you go, no matter how difficult the problem or unique the circumstances, there is someone there trying to solve that specific problem and help people."

There is nothing more beautiful to see and more satisfying to experience than real people helping real people. This is especially the case when people have identified a specific segment of need and focused on it with all their resources. To obtain zero defects in our work, we must focus on requirements that are realistically within the scope of our resources. A small group of people in a suburban community cannot eliminate poverty or homelessness. They can, however, meet some of the specific requirements of poor or homeless people and do it right every time.

One of my clients operates a shelter for the homeless. She told me about a man she knows who regularly shows up outside her shelter late at night to provide food and drink for those who did not make it into the overcrowded shelter. When it is cold outside, the coffee is steaming hot; when it is hot and humid, the drinks are ice cold. The food is always served with personal care and love. Within the scope of his mission, he regularly functions without defects. He has determined what he can do very well and consistently meets those requirements with exceptional accuracy.

The lady who runs the shelter has a different agenda. Each evening after the doors are closed and the tables cleared away from dinner, she and her volunteers spend time with her guests. They care about every person, but they are looking for some who meet some very specific requirements. She knows from experience what to look for and how to measure human potential. She can quickly tell if the problems are too big for her to handle or whether her program of restoration will fit. She is making correct and proper judgments, not about a person's worth, but about whether the individual is able to do, with help, all that is necessary to overcome homelessness. She prayerfully and tearfully makes these decisions daily and uses her limited resources to provide comprehensive case management for a few. When the situation calls for only food and rest, she does it with a zero defects attitude. She strives to do the right thing for each client, every time.

This concept of qualifying clients creates some anxiety among nonprofit managers until they understand how much time, energy, and money they waste doing the wrong things. The failure to qualify clients and to know what services are reasonable for the circumstances can be one of the greatest misuses of resources. It is a difficult issue in nonprofit management, but one that must be confronted honestly. When you improperly apply resources by ordering surgery because you were reluctant to determine whether or not a bandage would work, you are probably depriving someone else of much needed surgery or denying hundreds who need only a bandage.

One example of this reluctance to qualify clients showed up in a counseling center at which I was consulting. They regularly referred their clients for professional help and paid for the services out of contributed funds. I recommended they determine which of the clients had insurance that could be billed by the professional counselor for the service provided. They resisted, not wanting to discuss money with their clients and appear to be insensitive. Their resistance dissolved when I pointed out they were paying the bill for many who could pay, while turning away those who could not pay because the organization had spent its money unwisely. A defect-free organization must create practical strategies for service that press beyond rhetoric.

Chapter Review

Quality improvement requires changes in thinking and behavior in our individual and organizational lifestyles. The dilemma most people encounter in setting new standards for service is deciding whether they should give up the standards that already exist. The manager who is committed to improving the quality of services must deliberately probe the depths of his or her motivations, management style, and philosophies of service. *Make a list of those topics in this book that have disturbed you as you have read them and keep them handy as you progress through the improvement process. Add to them or check them off as you find new ones and eliminate others.*

Although the principles of quality management lead us to reexamine our methods and motivations for service, they represent far more than what motivational techniques alone can achieve. In quality management, we are applying practical principles to processess and causing lasting change. The results create enthusiasm for change and improvement that no motivational technique can produce. Nearly everyone can recall the results of some motivational experience in their life that was ultimately disappointing. *Take a few minutes now to write out those experiences and consider how they were different from what quality management promises.*

Every volunteer, staff member, or manager should consider why they do their work the way they do it and how they can do it better. This is particularly important for those who establish policies and procedures because the whys definitely affect the hows. Not all things done in the name of mercy or compassion are necessarily motivated by those traits. Some are the result of a person's need for acceptance or of a personal bias that influences the ability to provide rational leadership. A misguided sense of compassion and caring can drain mercy away from the place of greatest need. You may recall a time when you have seen this happen. *Describe what the cost of doing things wrong was in that situation.*

The commonly held ethical and moral limits of only a couple of decades ago no longer constrain some of us in the delivery of services. Whether we are thinking clearly and accepting or rejecting new ideas affects our struggle between new principles and previously held ones. Although some obviously highrisk management styles are properly resisted by nonprofit managers, I have often consulted with people who have struggles with routine business discipline and self-organization because of inappropriately held nonprofit economic theories or attitudes about material management. Where conflict arises in your thinking, remember to refer to your list of disturbing topics. In each case you will need to reflect on the conflict and come to a place of clear thinking.

When some people think of improving the quality of their organization's services and eliminating the causes of errors, they mistakenly think of achieving perfection. The concept of zero defects is not the same as perfection. In fact, it is significantly different. Zero defects is the performance standard established for a process by any person who wants to do things right every time and not present a client with a service that is defective or incomplete in any way. It is reasonable to expect that people will make mistakes and that improvement will come gradually. It is just as reasonable for zero defects to be your standard of quality. *Write down the reasons given why this is true.*

Establishing supplier standards can have a dramatically positive effect on your ability to improve services. Whether your supplier is providing purchased or contributed goods and services, they should meet specific requirements before they are paid for or receipted. Substandard supplies and suppliers create extra work and poor morale. In the case of professional services, their failure to perform can be devastating to your organization.

Volunteers supply much needed human resources that when properly engaged can be worth tens of thousands of dollars in conserved personnel costs to even the smallest organizations. On the other hand, volunteers who are poorly introduced to an organization's processes can create chaotic inconsistency in services and quickly offset any gains provided by their services.

Even clients must sometimes be qualified by service standards so that we know best how to serve them and fulfill our objectives. You may have had experiences where failure to establish standards for suppliers, volunteers, or clients was costly. *Describe what the price of nonconformance was in those situations.*

5

Quality and Entrepreneurship: The Marketing Edge

When the IRS designates an entity as nonprofit and exempt from taxes, it is not mandating that it must be unprofitable.

Public Entrepreneurship

The nonprofit world is generally hesitant to encourage entre-preneurship as a competitive force of enterprise. There are, however, thousands of individuals using their entrepreneurial skills to organize and develop new nonprofit organizations. They take all the personal risks and responsibilities of a for-profit ven-ture with few personal rewards. They create, design, and inno-vate to bring to birth new organizations and services, only to find themselves bogged down in a quagmire of management limitations. Once the initial organizational phase is completed, nonprofit managers commonly slip into environmentally induced management drowsiness.

This story about a game of nonprofit management pro-vides a picture of this process. Team A comes into the game rated as as underdog. We will identify the nonprofit entrepreneur with Team A. People everywhere are telling Team A that their opponent is overwhelmingly strong, but their coach thinks they can make a difference. Against all odds, the coach has obtained a charter to enter the league, called together a team of players, borrowed, begged, and personally financed to get the team's equipment, and held practices. In Team A's case, the fact that they are practicing together fuels their enthusiasm. Their opponent will be Team B, which represents the long-term challenge to their success.

From the opening kickoff, Team A dominates every aspect of the game by using all of its entrepreneurial and innovative skills. The coach draws upon past business experience and successes in enterprise to create a momentum that the spectators recognize. They begin to cheer for Team A and offer their support as the team rolls to a healthy lead at halftime.

When the members of Team A return to the dressing rooms, they find several "friends" there to greet them and to offer their counsel for the second half. They comment on how well the team members have used their business skills and experience but caution them to remember that they are "nonprofit." Besides that, they are not sure some of the plays used were "legal." They recommend a more traditional approach to the game which is not as aggressive but will surely provide a more appropriate appearance for this "nonprofit" environment. Their counsel includes ways for the team to secure the victory won in the first half without risking it in the second half. With all of this input, Team A returns to the field.

The second-half strategy makes the Team A coach uncomfortable, but rather than go against "experienced" counsel and risk major complications, he chooses to follow the recommendations. The game becomes sluggish and unspectacular. Team A slowly loses its momentum and psychological advantage, while Team B appears to grow more intimidating and whittles away at Team A's lead in scoring. Team A begins to call on the spectators for more support, but they have become less enthusiastic as they have watched Team A's efforts dissipate. It is late in the fourth quarter when Team A's coach realizes that he must do something different to win.

The thing we never know is whether it is too late to recover from poor economic or management theory. We do know that it takes management that understands its options and is enterprising. Breaking out of the trap of traditional nonprofit thinking requires the same entrepreneurial risk taking as starting up the organization in the first place. The manager who succeeds in overcoming the traditional limitations placed on nonprofit administration will endure naysaying, scowling, and foot dragging along the way by well-intentioned friends. He or she must have the personal vision to know what needs to be done and conviction about how to do it.

Learning to Compete

Some nonprofit managers like to think of themselves as existing in an environment where there is no competition. Among other things, that can mean they think no one else is providing the same services in their community or that there is not a spirit of competition between nonprofits. Where there are others providing the same service, cooperation between organizations is generally the factor described as evidence of the absence of competition. Each of these examples can result in a management style that causes the organization to be vulnerable to the competition that does exist. Services are also managed well below their quality potential. Competition makes us all work better. When we convince ourselves that there is no competition in our marketplace, we deceive ourselves.

The idea that you might be the only nonprofit organization in your community providing the service that you do may not be accurate. In some cases it is obvious who your competitors are, but many times two or three nonprofits can exist in even a small community and not be aware of one another's presence. As a grantmaker, I have done site visits where the grantseekers declared with pride that they were the only ones providing the specific service described. To their amazement I would tell them about another nonprofit, sometimes not too far down the street, with an identical service in its portfolio *and* which the foundation I represented had already supported financially. There may be several reasons this can happen, but in my opinion, it is because the organization does not have a community-wide vision.

There are always more clients in a community than there are services. Because of this, the competition is not for clients but for contributors. Remember, in the for-profit world where there are paying customers, competitors always appear on the scene to share the profits. In the nonprofit world, people who want to do good are always ready to share your community's contributors.

Service providers tend to generate their financial support through the network of their relationships. Since another network can exist alongside yours without crossing in most spots, there is not competition for every contributor. The places where the two networks will most likely cross over is at the addresses of the largest contributors in your area. There, competition exists. Large gift contributors who have relationships with one or more service providers must make decisions about how to divide the contribution pie.

There are two ways nonprofit organizations might be expected to compete — rhetoric versus rhetoric, or quality versus rhetoric. When it is rhetoric versus rhetoric, you can easily go out of business. When you emphasize quality versus rhetoric, you will more likely succeed and gain a larger share of contributions. The only way to deal effectively with competition is to be the best service provider in your community.

I have a client whom I have counseled in organizational development for several years. She works with children who are born blind, deaf, or with some other neural deficiency. She is both a scientist and a nurturer. Her methods have been recognized on an international scale and the results of her work are astonishing. Her competitor's operation was designed around sensationalism. There was little science, nurturing was inconsistent, and the organizational scheme was nearly inverse to what it should have been. The competitor, however, was an enthusiastic salesman of his operation.

On the level of rhetoric, the competitor was able to manipulate important contributors in the community through what I considered to be unethical fund-raising techniques. He was so good at it that contributors were submitting joyfully to the experience. He had eaten into the contribution base of my client and had used deliberate attacks on her mission to obtain funding advantages.

My client decided to forgo the war of rhetoric and to concentrate on the quality of her work. She refused to retaliate or to allow any of her board members, staff, or clients' parents to do so. She focused her organization's time and energy on the design and improvement of service. For some time the competitor moved about freely, taking advantage of the apparent noncombativeness of my client. Despite this, my client pressed on toward improving her work while reasonably maintaining her contributor base. One by one, contributors became aware of the rhetorical onslaught and began to do their own site visits and make their own comparisons. The competitor who relied on rhetoric eventually went out of business. Quality triumphed again.

Surviving to Serve

The day-to-day struggle most nonprofit managers must endure to meet operational expenses is well known. In addition to the hard work of providing services to their clients, they must concentrate much of their energy into finding new contributors as well as maintaining the ones they already enjoy. The emotional load of this regime takes its toll on managers and staff. Human problems that would be routinely handled under less demanding circumstances can escalate and multiply into a crisis that consumes energy and time. The situation is similar to that which a family experiences when it is under financial strain. It is difficult to stay focused on individual family needs when the resources are low and the bill collectors are pounding away at your patience.

It is during times like this that the self-discipline of quality management pays off. Whether you are the head of a family receiving financial counsel or a nonprofit manager designing a plan for recovery, the place to start is to list the requirements that must be fulfilled to remain in operation. As the list grows, some items will stand out as irrelevant or unimportant to the realities of survival. It is interesting how we can hold on to things and justify their expense until we get to the point of choosing what is important to survive.

Some strategic planners have labeled this process as coming to a "war footing." When we declare war, we begin to reassess the importance of all resource-consuming assets — each plan or process within our organizational structure and the financial liabilities of every decision. We become conservationists in the management of all our resources and painlessly discard options that do not fit the agenda. The nonprofit manager who has discovered the need to improve the quality of client services or to restructure the balance between patronage and profitability must lead his or her organization into a war-footing preparedness.

Because processes are moving and alive, they are dynamic. They carry with them energy, talent, and focus. Bringing processes into balance begins with eliminating those that are destructive in nature and limit the fulfillment of our operating requirements. Others must be modified to remain useful. Each process must be measured by how it causes the operational requirements to be fulfilled.

There are some processes that can be harnessed together to produce greater efficiency. One excellent example would be the harnessing of public enterprise to patronage in order to fulfill budget requirements. One complements the other. Another might be the harnessing of the improvement of client services to the development of patronage. Two processes might complement each other directly and also harness easily to other pairings. Quality management brings processes into a place where effective pairings can be accomplished. As each process is added, eliminated, or modified to conform with the operational requirements, it will become easier to pair them together.

Every nonprofit organization is unique. In order to find the mix of initiatives and processes that will further your particular goals, you must first bring your organization to a war footing. Then the steps of defining requirements, committing to standards, designing measurements, and evaluating performance can begin. In this war, winning is surviving. The purpose of quality management is to win the war and keep it won day to day.

Fulfilling the Mission

Every operational activity of a nonprofit organization should be focused on fulfilling the requirements set forth in the mission statement. I have mentioned before the importance of a well-defined mission statement. Unless it reflects the actual requirements of your community and the special clientele you intend to serve, it cannot be useful in directing your efforts or focusing on quality improvement.

Even routine board meetings and staff discussions run more smoothly when the requirements of the organization and that specific meeting are well established. What manager has not experienced a runaway meeting? The useless processes that are doing nothing for your mission statement and wasting resources were probably born in runaway meetings. Sometimes a trustee or strong-willed contributor seizes an opportunity to ask that his or her special concern be considered as part of the organization's portfolio of services. If your mission statement and operating requirements are not well defined, and your agenda is not well established, you risk embarrassment or loss of the ability to redirect the meeting back to its purpose. Eliminating these events is simple and risk-free when the first response becomes "let's look at our requirements." Let the organization's requirements be your sergeant-at-arms.

The mission statement becomes the standard by which everything else is established. It should be changed only after much thought, discussion, and reflection. The portfolio of services each organization supports should be the result of assessing its mission and requirements. When you are reorganizing for quality improvement, assessments must begin with the mission statement and continue through each individual service in the portfolio. In that way you can eliminate, modify, or create processes to fulfill your mission instead of writing a mission statement to ordain what you are already doing.

Whether you are restructuring fund-raising efforts or adding new enterprises, the mission statement should remain as the guidepost for your enthusiasm and innovation. Every client service and process should be specifically designed to fulfill requirements and to receive the full attention of the leadership and staff in applying effective business administration. The result should be activities that create appropriate services and the finances to support them.

The types of enterprise that are conducive to the fulfillment of the mission statement and can generate financial resources fall into four basic categories. For this discussion, we are excluding patronage through contributions which, of course, should be enterprising. The nonprofit that is managing for quality should become enterprising in all that it does.

Enterprises that have consumer and commerical appeal and do not depend on a contribution motive are the most common. They can range from the sale and distribution of products or services during a specific annual time frame to recreational and entertainment activities with broad public appeal. Solid commercial structuring of the enterprise is primary. Exposure of the organization to the community is a secondary benefit.

Client enterprises that involve the creation of employment opportunities for underemployed or traditionally unemployable clients are a practical way to meet the social and financial needs of your clientele and underwrite the delivery of services. The range of manufacturing, sales, and service options is almost unlimited.

Commercial enterprise related to your mission involves the profitable application of the talents, services, or market demographics of your organization or its broad constituency. This could mean that you sell the same service to individuals or corporations that you are giving to those who cannot pay. It could also involve the creation of additional products or services, using existing talents and skills related to your mission.

Unrelated commercial enterprises are business activities with no relation to your mission and with only one objective, to produce profits for your mission. This income could become subject to taxes but would not necessarily affect other tax-exempt activities or privileges. Unrelated activities should only be attempted when the measurable profitability is significant, the probability of success is high, and the risk of drawing away organizational energy is low. Managing an enterprise that is not related to your mission's activities carries great risks in splitting the focus of your work. Again, the mission statement becomes the best measure of what enterprises are appropriate. The possibilities are innumerable.

Improving on Success

Before services are added to the existing portfolio or enterprise options are installed, quality management should become the organizational routine. Implementing quality management concepts and new services or enterprises simultaneously could be something like trying to learn the piano and guitar at the same time. The special disciplines of each would be too much for most people to accomplish. However, after learning the piano and becoming comfortable with its demands, many people find the addition of other instruments to be somewhat less demanding.

Quality management directly challenges the cultural and environmental norms of any nonprofit organization. It creates a renewed understanding of the value and practicality of management processes. An enterprising and profitable approach to management grows along with the development of the improvement processes. The result will be a major restructuring of economic and management theory for most participants and will require all the energy, patience, and teaching ability of the manager. It would overload the reasonable performance expectations of most organizations to try to accomplish additions of services or enterprises until the disciplines, language, and routines of quality management are solidly in place.

We cannot accelerate the acquisition of quality improvement principles beyond our ability to learn the theory and then practice it in daily processes. The repetitions are necessary to instill the change in cultural norms. While these human processes can deteriorate when they are accelerated, there are some specific steps that can be taken to rid the educational process of unnecessary interference and streamline the procedure.

Eliminating services and processes that do not fulfill the mission statement is the place to start. Trying to practice quality management on processes that do not produce outcomes that meet the client's requirements is bad business. Not only that, such a process is not "pairable" to other processes that are meeting the requirements and will impede quality improvement. It is like trying to inflate a whale with a bicycle pump. The whale is not likely to cooperate and its basic design is wrong anyway.

Put your efforts into those areas of service and into processes that are already fulfilling requirements. You must tie quality improvement to the processes you know you must have to survive. That is where you can see immediate results. The savings in wasted resources when unneeded processes are eliminated will give your budget a shot in the arm as well. Do not fall prey to the mentality that cutting back is losing ground. Think of it as excess fat and asset-consuming activity.

While you are bringing current processes under the discipline of quality management, you can begin to define those services and processes you will need to add. New enterprises and services should be carefully planned before they are "paired" with other processes. Before resources are committed to new activities, the marketing and timing questions must also be thoroughly explored.

Measuring Markets

One of the things that will become clear to you as you embrace these concepts is the need to be aware of your environment. The attitudes, ideas, and philosophies of those around you must be clearly perceived and understood. When improvement is the focus of your management style, you cannot afford to be uninformed about the way your various constituencies think. Your staff, volunteers, contributors, and clients all have valuable insights into the processes of your organization that can provide the critical adjustments you want to achieve. The process of providing a service to a client does not exist in a vacuum. People's needs change. People's attitudes change as well. To be effective, the manager must be in a place of perspective where changes are perceived and analyzed as a routine of management. It is a concept that is fundamental to marketing.

I was sharing some of these thoughts with a friend once when he cringed and said, "I know you didn't mean it that way, but it sounds so commercial, so businessy when you say market." I responded by explaining to him that a market is a group of people who think or act in certain ways. How they will behave in relation to what you have to offer them is a very important thing to know. You want to present your offer to them in an appealing way so that they will understand your good intent. Whether it is the clientele you want to serve or the contributor you need to convince, knowing who will listen and respond favorably and why they will do so is critical to the success of any endeavor.

In the nonprofit world, when markets have demonstrated their positive response to your entreaty, they are sometimes called constituents. But the real answer to my friend's challenge was more direct. Yes, I did mean to say market and no, it is not too "businessy." If you must cringe, I hope it is because you realize that you have ignored this important element of management and now see its necessity. Being aware of the way your clients and contributors think and feel is another way of saying you are sensitive to your market.

People's ideas and opinions change rapidly in today's mass media environment. With television and radio talk shows, print media, and network television news competing for the same audiences, we are bombarded with the latest ideas or opinions. As we watch, read, and listen, our opinions are reshaped. How we respond today may be quite different from what yesterday's response would have been. Because of this rapid-fire input and change process, instead of two opinions—"yes" or "no" being the primary divisions on a subject—we may find our responses divided by the "what ifs" and "why nots" into many segments.

Much of life is broken into segments. In business we sometimes find that instead of large and constant markets, we have several smaller ones that are quite likely to change. Each segment of our total market must be carefully approached and specifically stimulated with the idea that is important to that group. We also need to stay aware of developing attitudes and ideas so that our presentation remains within the current scope of our market's reality. Segmenting the same service or skill to several smaller markets is not only a practical way to obtain additional constituents, it also reduces the organization's vulnerability to sudden shifts of a large market.

A recovery program for alcoholics might be segmented as follows:

- To individual clients unable to pay for services, a treatment process financed by contributions
- To individual clients who are able to pay, a process financed by sliding-scale fees or third party (insurance) billing
- To corporate clients who are willing to underwrite some or all of their employees' expenses, individual or group processes on or off the corporate campus
- To government entities who will contract for educational and treatment processes within their operational staff or community
- To educational institutions who will contract for awareness seminars and counseling

The number of segments is limited only by your marketing creativity and how many you can manage.

Exchanging Value for Value

The principle of reciprocity is one that weaves its way through many parts of life. We give love in hope of receiving love. We work for someone in expectation of a wage or salary. The idea that there should be some exchange of value in relationships is certainly not a new one. What value you intend to give for value received must be clearly thought out and concisely presented to each market segment.

Of course, the one clear exception to the exchange of values is the client who is unable to reciprocate. It is a fundamental premise of charity and benevolence that we give to those who cannot return our gift. The freedom we have under tax-exempt law enables us to have a reciprocal relationship with those who can pay so that we can help those who cannot. Although our client may not be able to reciprocate financially, we gain in satisfaction and appreciation when we do our work well. The nonprofit motive is rooted in religious and social values that consider the individual who is unable to help himself or herself as the primary object of our efforts.

When we solicit individuals and corporate entities for contributions, we are operating in reciprocity. The contributor is looking for people who can perform a task on his or her behalf for a third party. Contributors have a need to give on the basis of personal, civic, or religious motives. Our way of exchanging values with contributors is to accomplish our task effectively and efficiently on their behalf. We must meet the needs of our clients and steward our contributors' finances with wisdom and integrity. When we enter into exchanging promises, we must know which community needs the contributor considers to be important and which motive guides his or her actions.

When clients who can pay come to nonprofit organizations for help, they are motivated by very specific requirements. Since they do have the ability to pay, they usually have other professional options at their disposal. So why would a client pay a nonprofit for a service it could pay for somewhere else? The answer is simple. In the client's opinion, that particular organization will meet his or her individual requirements better than the other options. The organization must know what factors represented in its service delivery structure are important to those people who have the ability to pay and the choice to make. Professionalism, personal care, and concern for the client, special counseling options, clinical setting, geographical location, price, and other variables can affect the final choice.

The for-profit employer who contracts with a nonprofit for services is inevitably concerned with the bottom line or profitability of his or her organization. It may manifest in concern about lost productivity, benefits for employees, or the ability to meet hiring requirements. This is particularly true in situations where substance abuse or child care is the nonprofit's specialty. However, the service could be personal financial counseling, nutrition, physical fitness, skills training, G.E.D. classes, or a myriad of other educational and self-improvement themes. As always, market research is essential in knowing what a company's needs are and who makes the decision.

Government entities may be acting on behalf of their employees or particular taxpayer needs. In each case, you must become aware of the specific needs of the organization, the political processes, and who will make the decision. To obtain this knowledge, you must deliberately and systematically communicate with entities targeted for marketing.

All of these processes start internally. You must decide what it is you do well and reach a level of consistency in the quality of your services that will allow you to approach new markets with confidence. Once you have outlined and categorized the processes that your organization has mastered, you can begin to look in various market segments for additional applications of the skill. Opportunities will arise where you have consulted with a potential client and realize that with only minor adjustments to your service delivery system you can meet that client's special needs. Conversely, creating special services for a potential client that would require significant restructuring of your skills could prove to be not worth the risk. It will always be more profitable for you to improve on your successes and market what you do best.

Helping For-Profits

Nonprofit and for-profit corporations can sometimes form relationships to share resources and achieve their individual corporate goals. There are circumstances in which the for-profit corporation's survival may be dependent on the nonprofit's ability to apply its special skills with people. Likewise, the nonprofit can benefit from the for-profit corporation's financial resources.

Nonprofit organizations are generally more knowledgeable about the fulfillment of human need and the restoration of human value than for-profit entities because they have been concerned about human need more intensely and for a longer period of time. Those in the for-profit world have become more aware of the complexities of managing their human resources but, many times, find themselves unable to do much more than help define the problem.

This is particularly true as the for-profit world assesses its future work force needs. Just about anywhere you turn in management circles people are lamenting the lack of qualified workers at entry-level positions, a situation that has already reached critical levels and may become catastrophic in the years ahead. The requirements that major employers have for recruiting potential employees are difficult, if not impossible, to meet in large numbers.

Employers must be sure that employees are trustworthy and above reproach in their personal contacts with customers. With the rising crime and drug abuse statistics, it is getting much more difficult to find potential employees who are not using or have not used illegal drugs. Time-consuming and expensive steps are taken to determine employee honesty in an effort to eliminate every potential liability to the employer.

The high-tech nature of even the most simple business processes is also adding difficult obstacles to the entry-level opportunities of the work force. An alarming number of applicants are unable to complete a basic employment application because of illiteracy. Their potential for learning technical procedures or for operating equipment becomes less probable because of their inability to read manuals and communicate in written form.

When corporate managers decide not to use anyone who is illiterate, has an arrest record, or cannot pass a drug test, they may be trying to do the right thing the wrong way. I am aware of situations where employers have interviewed tens of thousands of potential employees, trying to find one thousand who meet the requirements, only to give up trying to fill the jobs. The costs of the interviews, medical exams, credit research, and paperwork needed to manage these activities are enormous. What is more important, the results are frequently very unfavorable. It is obviously not good business to spend millions of dollars in personnel costs testing and researching applicants only to find out that they are unemployable. Since the need for entry-level employees is growing and the labor pool is generally getting worse not better, employers must become more practical.

This unfortunate condition in the marketplace has created huge opportunities for nonprofit enterprise. Nonprofits are specialists in nearly every form of human restoration. They can assess human problems, diagnose causes, and move individuals through constructive processes with remarkable skill. They routinely provide employment counseling and job-search services and are involved in nearly every conceivable form of education. An enterprising nonprofit could find that a contractual relationship to provide rehabilitated employees who meet special requirements, to supply educational or rehabilitative services for entry-level trainees on behalf of an employer, or to train human resource administrators in these areas might be quite easy to accomplish.

Recognizing Differences

Nonprofit organizations offer the greatest challenge and opportunity to the person who wants his or her life's work to count for something on the social scale but enjoys the processes of business. For many years, I wondered where I could find the total satisfaction I now experience applying my skills and talents in nonprofit administration. Business has always had its place in my heart, but my social agenda and concern for other people would never let me fully engage in the pure pursuit of business. That is certainly not to say that those who focus their lives on business are wrong. They are just different.

Recognizing individual differences is essential to the management of any organization. I have seen two different management styles accomplish the same objective and two entirely different organizations serve the same constituency with equal success. I have also seen management demand conformity without obtaining the singular and homogeneous output expected. It is difficult, if not impossible, to apply any principle uniformly across all organizational structures or management environments. Because of the unique experiences, education, and personality of every staff member, volunteer, and manager, there will be variation in how the elements we have discussed will ultimately manifest in the delivery of services, enterprise, and overall performance. Some people will decide they need to boost one area of performance while others will get an entirely different message.

One of the areas of individual difference that should be highlighted because of its effect on a total management environment is the comparative strengths of what I call entrepreneurial and custodial administrators. Knowing which you are will be useful in understanding the types of management decisions you make. It will also help you to see your need for the managerial strengths of other people in your organization.

Custodial managers are people with an unusual capacity to steward successfully the essential parts and details of a process. They can see the big picture and can contribute strategic insight, but they are most happy when they are allowed to work closely with a process and experience it in depth on a daily basis. They draw energy from the regularity and demanding nature of processes. They can pull away and perform entrepreneurial activities, but only for short periods of time.

Likewise, the entrepreneurial administrator can see and understand the work of the custodial administrator but finds it physically and emotionally exhausting to accomplish with regularity. The entrepreneurial administrator thinks statistically and strategically and has a naturally sequential approach to management. For his or her gifts to work effectively, this manager must stay at arm's length from the daily processes.

Neither the entrepreneurial nor custodial administrator will be able to exempt himself or herself completely from those responsibilities and activities most suited to the other. In fact, to do so would be a mistake. Each should force himself or herself to endure the other's environment at least 10 percent of each work week as a basic discipline of management. When either loses appreciation for the other or operates without a current understanding of the other's work, a gap in organizational sensitivity will exist that will skew perceptions and decisions out of reality. The stewardship of nonprofit processes is improved

Quality and Entrepreneurship: The Marketing Edge   101

when the correct balance of skills and authority in these clearly different but interdependent management styles is attained.

The Gala Fund-Raiser

Knowing who you are as a person and understanding the value of your skills within an organization can make a big difference in how effectively your time is spent, especially if you are a volunteer board member. I have often talked with trustees and board members who make the mistake of trying to work in a nonprofit environment without the benefit of their for-profit skills. They place themselves under the confinement of a role expectation that is neither natural nor reasonable.

Seated next to me on a commercial airline flight one afternoon was a woman who was eager to tell me about the volunteer work she did for a very worthy nonprofit in her hometown. She was a certified public accountant and was obviously sophisticated and experienced in business processes. She was responsible for the oversight of several major commercial operations around the Eastern seaboard and regularly made financial and operational audits of very complex enterprises for her employer.

The woman's business exploits were well known to her fellow board members at the place where she volunteered, so they quickly appointed her chairperson of the annual fund-raising gala. She accepted the responsibility, generously pouring her time and energy into the project, which was a lawn party that had been institutionalized into the organization's annual calendar. Since the organization's budget had been stretched to the limit, the new trustee was eager to make the event a financial success.

As she described the organizational processes of the project, I could see that her interaction with the staff was one of the highlights of her experience. She described with glowing pride the wonderful work the dedicated staff members accomplished and how inspiring it was to see them sacrifice prosperity and social position to help the less fortunate. She told me of the telephone calls she had made to a long list of friends and business associates describing the organization's special occasion and asking them to attend or participate in various ways. She had completed her assignment and successfully managed the gala event, which had now become her annual responsibility.

Later in our conversation, she solemnly began to express disappointment about her inability to involve some normally dependable associates in her nonprofit work and about the poor financial results of the event. I realized that her first description of the event had been the positive report she thought was expected of her, but that she was desperately looking for a way to work through her inner confusion about the experience.

As I questioned her, I began to see that her true feelings about the potential success of the event had been dominated by an intense desire to do what was pleasing to her friends in the organization. When asked if she knew why the event had not been a financial success, she answered only "I guess." When she told me how much, or actually how little, money the event had produced, her countenance dropped once again. Her next comment was most revealing: "They said I did better than last year."

She was very unhappy with the results of her work, and no amount of praise by her nonprofit associates could make her feel better. At her request, we backtracked over the performance of the event and began to estimate the total volunteer hours expended. Before I could complete my calculations, she had jumped mentally to the bottom line. Her business experience and expertise had been telling her all along that the event would fail financially. The two dollars per volunteer hour earned by the event was only one indication of something she had known was true but had not conveyed to her associates. She had expended hundreds of hours of labor on a bad project that would never fulfill its expectations. Although it was enterprising, it was not a good enterprise to attempt. She knew it and so did the business friends whom she had been unable to involve in the project.

She had failed to help the organization the way it really needed to be helped, and the way she was best equipped to help, by leading it away from an obviously unproductive event into fruitful enterprise. We wondered together how many other volunteers have done the same.

Chapter Review

Nonprofit entrepreneurs create, design, and innovate for the public good, often taking the risks of a for-profit venture without the same promise of returns. Sometimes the spectacular leadership that is demonstrated in the initial stages of development dwindles as the influences of traditional thinking begin to have their effect. Recapturing the entrepreneurial leadership that started an organization can become the critical force in the improvement of processes and services.

The nonprofit world is hesitant to encourage entrepreneurship beyond the basic innovation or development of new ideas and generally avoids the concept of competition. When nonprofit managers say there is no competition in their work, they usually mean that there are no other service providers in their area or that they have a cooperative relationship with one another. The nonrecognition of competition can result in a management style that causes an organization to manage well below its quality potential. Competition makes us all work better. There are two ways to compete: rhetoric versus rhetoric, or quality versus rhetoric. The only way to effectively deal with competition is to be the best service provider in your community.

When nonprofit organizations are under financial strain and need to design plans for recovery, the place to start is to list the requirements that must be fulfilled to remain in operation. It is interesting how we can hold on to things and justify their expense until we get to the point of choosing what is important to survive. Some strategic planners have labeled this as coming to a "war footing." The nonprofit manager who has discovered the need to improve the quality of client services or to restructure the balance between patronage and profitability must lead his or her organization into a war footing preparedness. *Make a list of the essential requirements your organization must fulfill.*

Every operational activity of a nonprofit organization should be focused on fulfilling the requirements represented in the mission statement. When you are reorganizing for quality improvement, assessments must begin with the mission statement and continue through each individual service in the portfolio. In that way you can eliminate, modify, or create procedures to fulfill your mission instead of writing a mission statement to ordain what you are already doing. The result should be activities that create appropriate services and the finances to support them. *Make a list of all the processes that are now operating in your organization. Do any of them stand out as wasting time and money?*

The nonprofit organization that is managing for quality should become enterprising in all that it does, including fundraising. There are, however, other enterprises conducive to the fulfillment of the mission statement that can generate financial resources. They fall into four basic categories:

- Enterprises that have consumer appeal and do not depend on a contribution motive
- Client enterprises that involve the creation of employment opportunities for underemployed or traditionally unemployable clients
- Commercial enterprises related to your mission that involve the profitable application of the talents, services, or market demographics of your organization or its broad constituency
- Unrelated commercial enterprises with no relation to your mission and with the sole objective of producing profits for your mission.

List some of the enterprises you might consider in each of these categories.

Before services are added to your existing portfolio or enterprise options are installed, quality management should become your organizational routine. By first eliminating processes that do not fulfill the mission statement, you can put your efforts into those processes you know you must have to survive. Then you can begin the process of measuring potential markets and learning how to apply your special skills in various market segments. To be successful, you will need to know the needs of each market so that you can exchange value for value and capitalize on the principle of reciprocity. Remember: ask, listen, think, and then do.

Recognizing individual differences is essential to the management of any organization. Custodial managers have an unusual capacity to steward the essential parts and details of a process. They draw energy from the regularity and demanding nature of processes. The entrepreneurial administrator thinks statistically and strategically, has a naturally sequential approach to management, but must stay at arm's length from daily processes. Whether you are a volunteer, staff member, or manager, it is essential to know how your gifts, talents, and personal managerial strengths can best serve your organization. *Make a list of the custodial and entrepreneurial managers in your organization. Compare the lists to the parties involved in past organizational conflicts.*

6

The Psychology of Quality: Eliminating the Obstacles to Improvement

The hindrances to quality improvement are often submerged in the myth and mystique of our culture.

Individual Psychology

Throughout this book, I have described attitudes, management styles, and cultural standards that my experiences have proven to be important in the teaching of quality management. There are also any number of concepts and beliefs that could limit our abilities to pursue quality. They are often found in our personal experiences and feelings as well as in traditional and cultural norms. In this chapter, I describe some of the more significant obstacles to quality improvement in a nonprofit culture and present a view of how they may be perceived by others.

The "psychology of quality" is a term I have used when I describe the process of finding and eliminating the emotional and cognitive obstacles to improvement. The positive motivation and commitment needed to pursue quality are an altogether separate issue. When you realize how attainable the benefits of quality can be, you may easily find the necessary motivation and commitment. Obstacles are those things that will interfere with your ability to sustain your improvement path. If I were to list some of the hindrances or obstacles to quality improvement, you might review the list and decide in all sincerity that you do not have "those particular problems." This is because they are not always easy to see, and you may have carried them for years unaware of their consequences. The difficulty lies in uncovering the hidden roots of resistance, the subliminal debates that can limit your success. The hindrances to quality improvement are often submerged in the myth and mystique of our culture. Even if you find that you are without significant hindrances in your own life and thinking, you will still need to be aware of the obstacles that may crop up in your work environment or in the lives of those you may want to influence toward quality management. Following are some important examples of such obstacles.

Management traditions include the things we learn directly and indirectly about management, and they have a great impact on our selection of business systems and initiatives. A lack of knowledge about the history of tax-exempt law and the emergence of the nonprofit sector is one of the more common intellectual obstacles to quality improvement. Although what we think we know about the law and what it requires of us may be completely inaccurate, we accept it because of traditional examples. If we believe that nonprofit organizations are not allowed to be profitable, it can have a dramatically limiting effect on our choices of language, methods, and enterprises. In regard to a manager's personal psychology, these things can set up a distinct resistance to the concepts of good business practice, profitability, and quality management.

Philosophical goodness can present one of the most subtle obstacles to the development of quality management principles in a nonprofit environment. To some people, the goodness of what they are doing is all that counts. When that is the case, the disciplines necessary to organize and deliver services of the highest quality may be difficult to achieve. An unrealistic emphasis on goodness, coupled with a resistance to the concepts of good business practice, can present an almost insurmountable obstacle to quality improvement. When we understand the commonality of goodness in nonprofit work, it can help to refocus some of our energy into management disciplines.

Social mystique accompanies philosophical goodness. It is a function of goodness in that it is an aura that surrounds the activities of nonprofit work. It is not a problem in and of itself, but it can become addictive and has the potential for masking a person's resistance to accountability and competent action.

The minority mentality poses one of the obstacles to quality that is hardest to overcome. It can represent a complex system of personal insecurities and individual personality needs, as well as a mixture of some of the cultural obstacles just described. It can be identified by several unique peculiarities that are described more thoroughly later in this chapter.

The benefits of the pursuit of quality are so valuable to a nonprofit organization that you may be puzzled by all the arguments you will encounter against practicing quality management. When this occurs, you will more than likely have touched someone's cultural or personal tender spot in a way that even he or she does not fully comprehend. The roots of resistance in someone's life may be entangled in education, training, and experiences that will require patient reexamination to uncover. That someone could even be yourself.

Management Traditions

Like so many other areas of law and management, the principle of tax exemption has its basis in ancient religious and societal norms. It has been affirmed over the centuries and has generally survived the tests of history and common sense. An organization that attains tax-exempt status is the beneficiary of a profound opportunity to apply entrepreneurship, compassion, and practicality in fulfilling social motivations while remaining exempt from any responsibility to underwrite the nation's infrastructure through taxes. We are exempt from these burdens because we operate under the public perception that what we do is important to society and that we are managing a business that provides services for reasons other than personal financial gain.

The word "nonprofit" may carry with it an inference about profit that causes some people to think profitability by a nonprofit organization is illegal. To the contrary, we are free to do anything a for-profit company might do as we pursue our goals, *including making profits.* The law is designed to provide all the benefits of a free-market system plus the special favor of tax incentives for individuals and corporations who want to contribute financially to our efforts. Not only can we operate enterprises profitably as tax-exempt organizations but we can also prosper through the patronage of others.

Prior to 1894, all entities, whether individual or corporate, were exempt from taxation under U.S. law unless they were named as being subject to a particular tax. The Tariff Act of 1894 subjected all corporations to a flat 2 percent tax rate with exemptions for nonprofit charitable, religious, and educational organizations. The important aspect of this legislation is that organizations involved in enterprise and whose profits would be used for altruistic purposes were specifically excluded from the requirement to share the profits of their work through taxation. The initial emphasis of tax exemption was to protect the enterprises of nonprofit organizations from taxation, and it has remained as the central function of tax-exempt law to this day. We are not expected to manage our business operations and mission activities differently from for-profit organizations as regards efficiency, quality, or substance. What the IRS is concerned with is the objectives of our work and the uses of our income.

Financial and legal professionals must carry a large part of the responsibility for the poorly conceived intellectual traditions concerning nonprofit profitability. It might surprise you to know that very few of these well-intentioned professionals that I meet have an accurate overall perspective of tax-exempt law or a clear understanding of important fundamentals. Because they are poorly prepared to provide counsel on tax-exempt law, they very often create negative and fearful images of the intent of our lawmakers. The pursuit of profit for personal or individual gain is called private enterprise. Profits gained through private enterprise are taxable. Enterprise by tax-exempt organizations has as its goal for attaining profits the continued provision of services for the public good. Profits earned from public enterprise related to our tax-exempt mission are not taxable. Nonprofit organizations can engage in virtually any business enterprise in the fulfillment of their mission objectives and remain comfortably within the purposes of their tax-exempt status. Where the enterprise is *unrelated* to the stated mission, *only* that income that is generated by the unrelated enterprise is taxable. Gifts, contributions, and income generated by another enterprise related to the organization's mission statement would remain tax exempt.

The pessimist, it is said, sees the glass as half empty and the optimist as half full. Consider this simple parallel. Some perceive contributions as the only legal option for financing their services and feel that enterprise is a foreign element in their work. Others see contributions as only one of the financial benefits of their tax-exempt status and believe that enterprising and disciplined business practices are central to achieving their goals. The motivational and management potential under the latter approach causes the manager to see the glass as half full and fillable. Using the principles of quality management, we can create better services for our clients and economic gains for our organization's needs.

Philosophical Goodness

Why we want to do good things for people has strong ties to our moral, ethical, and religious concepts of human value. In the United States, we are so eager to find expressions of human concern and to meet our social obligations that we have created an entire sector of society with specialized law to support its mission. Even though our efforts as individuals may sometimes conflict religiously, philosophically, or politically, we are committed as a society to the free expression of goodness through our nonprofit institutions.

I find my personal standards for morality, integrity, and goodness in the Bible. It also provides me with guidance for financial management, human relations, time management, and many other administrative concepts. In my case, the biblical standard provides a process for implementing not only my religious faith but also my professional standards and discipline. This works out very well for me personally, and I am comfortable with the expressions of goodness it allows. Dozens of religious faiths use all or part of the Bible for the structuring of their own expressions of goodness, sometimes with very different results. Historically, we have emphasized our differences rather than the fact that we are using the same book for moral and ethical guidance.

There are intellectuals and academicians who, although they have rejected religious faith as a personal choice, continue to see value in the biblical writings as an ancient document of societal concerns. Many of our principles of law and business are rooted in biblical standards. As a text, the Bible has withstood the test of time and remains for many a powerful influence in establishing norms for social goodness.

Many other religious documents and faiths also consider goodness as essential to their creed or doctrine. These have existed alongside Hebrew and Greek biblical standards for many centuries. In nearly all of them, concern for the less fortunate through acts of benevolence and charity is widely accepted as a basis for goodness.

Some individuals and societal groups find their basis for goodness in philosophy, nature, or other nonreligious forms. It is difficult, however, to find standards of goodness, whether they are considered ethnic, cultural, religious, philosophical, or intellectual, that are very far afield from one another. Goodness is not unique to any culture or part of society.

Because acts of goodness are so much in evidence in all of society and particularly in the nonprofit world, it is a little odd that we should take anything we do too seriously on the basis of goodness alone. Certainly, goodness is a supporting fiber of nonprofit work, but finding it threaded through your organization should not create a superior sense of purpose. Its presence in your behavior is no assurance that anything else you do is appropriate, honest, or effective. Goodness is difficult to measure and improving on goodness or expressing more goodness than someone else might prove to be futile. To rise above the rest, you need to improve the quality of the good things you do.

Social Mystique

The dictionary defines mystique as "a framework of doctrines, ideas, beliefs, or the like, constructed around a person or object, endowing him or it with *enhanced value* or profound meaning." A second definition is "an aura of mystery or mystical power surrounding a particular occupation or pursuit." There are many professions that enjoy a public perception of mystique. That special mystique enhances marketability and is many times deliberately created.

We lavish privilege and special honor on those whose professions are considered superior or of a higher social value. As that value is often measured in dollars, the probability that others will be impressed and mystified by what we do increases with the financial rewards. Another way in which value is measured is through the apparent goodness of what we do, especially by way of personal sacrifice for the benefit of others or by religious leadership. Rabbis, priests, and ministers have always enjoyed a special place of honor in the community.

I have chosen two measures of mystique to describe its power. There are probably several others, but it is what we do not know about a person or profession that primarily sustains mystique. In most cases, if we were to examine closely the daily routines of people's work, we would find little to be mystified about.

In one of my jobs in the aerospace industry, I was fortunate to be assigned to a group of scientist-engineers who, in our culture, enjoyed a mystique just slightly below that of the astronauts. They were called the "super-specialists" and they were an elite team of experts in various aerospace technologies. They provided the depth of experience and knowledge necessary to make decisions where "the book" had not been written. They routinely provided oversight to various launch team activities and were the final word in those individual processes.

My job was to be their "gofer" and obtain test data and other information they might need from various departments or subcontractors when they were troubleshooting a problem. Sometimes they did their work individually or with part of the team they supervised, but everyone knew that "the power was flowing" when the super-specialists were all working together on a problem. The mystique surrounding these professionals was astounding, and since I was regularly privileged to sit in their midst and listen to their corporate wisdom, I could see it was well deserved.

I later worked with a group of computer scientists who created the programs for the astronauts' flight simulators. Again, the mystique was considerable, but this time I was one of the group. It was obvious to me that, although all of us enjoyed the mystique, only a handful of us were expert enough to deserve that level of honor. There were real experts all around me. I did good work but was receiving the greater benefit of a group process, and I knew it.

I had several opportunities in engineering and business to observe and experience the effects of mystique, but not until I entered the nonprofit world did I fully understand its power. There is no more alluring social power on earth than the mystique of doing good. I could see that to enjoy it you needed no special education, credentials, or experience. Nor is it necessary for you to be especially efficient, organized, or effective at your task as long as it is perceived by others that you are trying to do good.

Many people have invested their lives in nonprofit work with an attitude of service and sacrifice that is based in the reality of their abilities. Unfortunately, the social mystique of doing good is so strong that being fully involved in nonprofit work is no indicator of individual motives or competence. Some individuals and organizations exist primarily on the basis of their abilities to market social mystique. Where people are relying heavily on social mystique for their success, it will be difficult to gain a commitment to quality management.

The Minority Mentality

When I use the term "minority mentality," I am not specifically referring to racial or ethnic minorities. In the nonprofit world, nearly all organizations serve a numerical minority or subgroup of society. For instance, one mission might be to serve those with a specific disease. The people with that disease are a numerical minority among all of a population or among all people with diseases. The minority mentality is a label I have ascribed to certain mind-sets and behavioral expressions that commonly surface among nonprofit minorities.

An organization with a minority mentality can eventually become so focused on making sure every other part of society is aware of its minority status, and in securing expressions of concern from them, that little or nothing is actually accomplished on behalf of its constituents. When our processes become affected by a minority mentality, we focus more on the saying than the doing. We lose sight of our stewardship responsibilities and do not fully capitalize on our enterprise opportunities. The outcome is that meaningless rhetoric is sowed and meaningless rhetoric is reaped. This happens when we allow the negative results of minority experiences to rule our lives. It causes us to have unreasonable expectations of society and to be oblivious to the fact that nearly all of us fit into some minority group with special needs.

Personal minority experiences properly integrated into a person's thinking and adult behaviors can be valuable assets that add credibility to the presentation of our mission. When they are presented along with the requirements of our clients and constituents, they can also provide a snapshot of the quality of our work on their behalf. Our testimony about certain conditions or needs our constituency endures which we have personally experienced can help a prospective supporter identify with us more closely. This is especially true where public opinion about our minority requires adjustment.

Certainly, no one chooses to act irresponsibly or ineffectively on behalf of his or her constituents. However, people whose behaviors are rooted in the minority mentality are apt to be less able to function according to specific mission requirements and more likely to indulge in substanceless rhetoric. When we are acting on the basis of a minority mentality, we may be sincerely trying to express the results of our accumulated life's experiences. It is, however, our responsibility as leaders to identify the types and causes of our behaviors that may be limiting to the fulfillment of our mission and eliminate them from our lives. Whether it will require pastoral or psychological counseling, the criticism of a close friend, or just honest introspection, personal improvement is crucial to corporate management. Our minority is depending on us.

Feelings of Rejection

Life's difficulties can offer even the most buoyant personality a burden of conflicts and confusion. Our earliest recollections of insecurity and rejection may go back to a time when we were infants and without the ability to understand our feelings. The fact that those feelings were real and lasting is proven daily in the offices of ministers, counselors, and psychiatrists. Our behaviors are shaped by experiences that many times are overlooked as insignificant until their effect is discovered in the debris of good intentions.

Dozens of books have been written about the influence of self-image on our adult behaviors and how we accumulate input from life's experiences both good and bad as our personality grows and is shaped. Nearly everyone can point to a particularly pleasant or unpleasant experience that permanently affected how they felt about themselves as a person. The deep feeling of goodness from a parent's love and affection is an example of an experience that has escaped many people, although for the most part that cold emptiness is never acknowledged.

A sense of rejection by society and the lack of personal opportunity are experiences common to minorities. Many subgroup members have experienced the feeling of rejection either by another minority or by a majority that is ignorantly unaware of their special circumstances. Beyond the generalized experiences of rejection, many can recall specific instances when they were personally assessed and rejected by another individual or group. Our greatest vulnerabilities exist with the special friend, teacher, or authority who crushes our tender souls. Whether the incident is intentional or accidental, real or just perceived, the resulting pain is no less damaging.

I have counseled hundreds of individuals who have pursued the cause of inappropriate behaviors and attitudes in their lives only to find, through prayer or introspection, that the behavior did not exist prior to an incident of rejection. The results of identifying the individual or situation and forgiving those involved can be astonishing. However, sometimes it is not so simple. The feeling of rejection that is produced repeatedly by our environment can become so much a part of our lives that we accept it as our personal fate. Amazingly though, no matter how hard life's repetitions try to convince us of our valuelessness, the human soul cocoons around our pain and fights back to survive.

I have had many personal "healing" experiences as I have thought back through my life to disengage from pain and poor behavior by forgiving those who have afflicted my soul. Some behaviors that at one time dominated my life no longer exist as an obstacle to success simply because I realized that the bad feelings I had about myself and others were rooted in my experiences of rejection. New friends are surprised when I tell them about the offensive and destructive behaviors that were at one time well known by my old friends.

The mechanisms that our mind can create to cope with pain and defend itself against further damage are myriad in number. Psychologists and psychiatrists have described and labeled them in various counseling theories widely accepted in the mental health profession. Some of them are so strong that the part of our brain that apparently knows what behaviors and attitudes are correct can be overwhelmed by another that demands the right to express long-standing frustrations and emotions.

When this conflict takes place in the marketplace, we can be completely unaware of the intensity of our reactions and the embarrassment we bring to our minority. Sometimes our styles of behavior are so commonly developed within our minority community that we not only fail to recognize them but we also have them reinforced and supported by others suffering the same pain. Again, our responsibility as leaders is to separate ourselves and our organization from these behaviors and to help our constituents find better ways to cope.

Attitudes, Language, and Behaviors

It is interesting to look across the span of behaviors of any minority community. Whether the individuals have become negative and defeatist or arrogantly superior in their outlook toward others, there are at least two attitudes that will consistently dominate those who are operating in the minority mentality: inordinate prejudice and the compulsive pursuit of a selfish agenda.

The person who is bound by a minority mentality can fluctuate wildly between paranoia about others' perceptions of who he or she is and anger accumulated from all the unprocessed rejection. Insecure people have a great need to express to others the intense feelings trapped inside them. Because their feelings separate them from people both individually and as a minority group, prejudices often become the rationales for their feelings of rejection. In some strange way, we convince ourselves of our own worth by devaluing others. This overwhelming need for self-value is also manifested in compulsive needs for self-gratification and recognition.

The minority mentality sometimes provides group identification in the form of language. Communities dominated by minority thinking have well-known and established "secret slang" that they use to express their prejudices. Certain minorities use slang to refer to another minority in a disparaging manner. There is also culturally based slang that enables its users to talk about sensitive or vulgar subjects without a sense of embarrassment.

The language of the minority mentality has a distinct melody that can be easily identified. In some minority communities, it is a musical intonation that emphasizes slang words. In other subgroups, it is identifiable only by its consistent presence as a theme for rhetoric. It is very often highly critical of others and quite conducive to transmitting prejudicies. Amazingly, the communities that operate in the slang of the minority mentality seem to think that others cannot hear and understand it. Several times I have shared with a minority group a few lines of their well-known slang and melody to their great surprise and embarrassment. When they realize how obvious it is to others, they remember that they usually switch back to commonly accepted language when outsiders are present. Becoming aware of how we compensate for our insecurity in this way might cause us to wonder how many times we have used minority language without realizing it.

In addition to attitudes and language, there are distinct behaviors that are associated with the minority mentality. These are sometimes integrated with language and attitude for full effect. The most common among them are the whining and preaching that support the rhetoric of the minority. These behaviors foster the accomplishment of group objectives through manipulation, guilt, and accusation — a classic fulfillment of the deny/accuse defense mechanism. They often manifest themselves within the service structures and fund-raising processes of an organization that is focused more on saying than doing.

Present at the meeting where I first shared these observations publicly was a well-known veteran of the minority's cause who had labored vigorously to bring attention to his constituents' needs. When I finished my presentation, this person jumped to his feet and began to exhibit in dramatic detail all of the attitudes, language, and behaviors I had just described to the audience about their group. He did so as he loudly and angrily told me how completely out of touch with their minority I must be to draw such conclusions. It was an astonishing moment of reality for all but one who attended.

Public Reactions

Picture yourself entering the world of corporate philanthropy in an effort to obtain financial grants for your organization from a local foundation or corporation. You have been relentless in your pursuit of an appointment with the grantmaker and have had political and business allies calling to encourage the grantmaker to meet with you and to give consideration to your grant request.

You prepare for your interview by compiling a scrapbook of your organization's philosophical goodness and the extreme needs of your minority. You have also practiced a flag-waving, join-the-crusade plea for support that will involve all the social mystique and political idealism you can muster. You are prepared to accentuate the presentation with the intensity necessary to move the grantmaker to a giving decision by providing personal testimony, horror stories, and victorious case histories. Finally, you will remind the grantmaker of his or her responsibility to your minority community. Unaware of how your behaviors are rooted in rejection and a minority mentality, you are ready to pull out all the stops.

The grantmaker is beset with his or her own set of attitudes and behaviors rooted in the many interviews conducted with organizations that behave as if they represent the only minority with a need. The grantmaker is accustomed to seeing grantees move in for the kill and has become suspicious of anyone who tries to enter into friendship. He or she has been through the flag-waving, desk-pounding, whining, and other grantee demonstrations dozens of times. The grantmaker has endured attempts to be manipulated by guilt, terrorized by political pressure, and seduced by philosophical goodness. He or she has progressed beyond the reach of these techniques and has become more than able to sit in cynical silence as the most powerful presentations are made. What you may not realize is that he or she is part of a special minority that has seen the raw underbelly of the nonprofit world and has survived to continue the search for effective investments.

I have just described one of many possible situations, among which there could be others more positive in nature. This scenario has been presented to demonstrate how the public might perceive manifestations of the minority mentality and how some circumstances tend to bring them into focus. You can use your imagination and draw from your personal experiences, but the probable outcome of this interview is less than promising.

Grantmakers do not have a predisposition to look upon manifestations of the minority mentality as cultural richness and diversity. These behaviors are neither positive nor objective in nature. Further, it is unrealistic to expect the corporate grantmaker to adjust unilaterally his or her own environment to help the minority. It does happen, but it is the exception rather than the rule. What the grantseeker is most likely to perceive and experience is more rejection. This debilitating cycle of grantsmanship is played out daily in the world of philanthropy. Grantseeking organizations have their prejudices confirmed through continued rejection as grantmakers continue to look for objective, honest, and viable representations of needs that they can fulfill. It can be very disheartening for everyone involved.

Rational Solutions

There are two roads to improvement that offer viable alternatives to these recurring collisions. The first option requires leadership on the part of the grantmaker in an "outside to inside" approach to the dilemma. It assumes that the organization's objectives are within the mission objectives of the grantmaker and that the grantmaker is inclined to mentor the manager. Of course, this requires a recognition by the manager of the grantmaker's good intentions and capabilities, providing a reasonable basis for an honest relationship.

The mentor must be able to provide loving acceptance of the manager and affirm his or her value while at the same time confronting the issues of the minority mentality. This is a difficult issue for many grantmakers who may not believe that close relationships with grantees are appropriate. Beyond that, certain individuals may lack the personal affinity to a particular grantee necessary to relate on terms of friendship. Whatever the situation, there must be the basis for mutual trust and respect between the parties.

It has been my experience that I can teach principles to people I do not know through lectures, but to mentor them, I must have a relationship. The leader with a minority mentality does not need another lecture. He or she needs a friend who will walk through the difficult passages of change. Lasting improvement will require the leader to recognize the behaviors that are inappropriate and how they manifest themselves in his or her personal life. He or she must then commit to eliminating those attitudes, behaviors, and language that are inappropriate. It is a rare experience when this happens in one or two encounters. This will take time, effort, and many loving repetitions of confrontation and correction. Each confrontation must be followed by time and opportunity for change before moving on to another item. The mentor must help the leader through these steps of improvement at a pace that reflects the strength of the relationship and the ability of the leader to change.

This process could involve technical assistance in the areas of business administration and communications, as well as opportunities for personal enrichment through seminars and study. Old behaviors that are recognized and rejected must be replaced by new ones through education and training. It is necessary for the leader to receive the support and education that will allow him or her to get beyond personal improvement and bring change to others.

The second option relies on the leader's recognition of the need for change and an "inside to outside" initiative. Beginning within, the leader must seek help from friends, associates, or professionals who can help identify and overcome the minority mentality. This might also be an opportunity for the leader to seek a grantmaking mentor who would commit to the time and resources required for improvement. The degree of difficulty encountered by the leader in analyzing and engaging in self-discipline will determine how much help from the outside is needed. Outside help can provide the perspective needed to prevent the leader from beginning to work on the staff and volunteers of the organization before his or her personal improvement is secured.

Both of these pathways begin with personal improvement for the leader and then broaden to the improvement of the organization as an entity. Quality improvement decisions will have lasting effects on the processes and activities of the organization when the leadership has taken responsibility for change and demonstrated improvement through personal example.

The Social Magnet

Because of elements like traditional thinking, goodness, and mystique, nonprofit organizations have a tendency to attract people who have the same concern or viewpoint as the leadership. These people may differ greatly in their individual tastes and personalities, but they usually share some very obvious characteristics. When constituents find they differ in their understanding but want to continue in the same work, they usually start their own organization. This selection process causes most nonprofits to end up with people who can work with commitment toward the same goals. This is one of the major strengths of nonprofit organizations and one of their primary weaknesses.

When people of like mind set their energies to fulfill a goal, wonderful things can take place. The ability to sacrifice personally for the common good is greatly facilitated when the working environment is in unity with the mission. This additional thrust to an organization's potential can sometimes be the factor that causes it to succeed when, by all accounts, it should have failed. The problem with this powerful and mystical force is that sometimes it makes it very difficult to refocus the organization. Again, this can be an asset unless there is a real need to refocus.

Many nonprofits have their origin in the individual experience of their founder. A person may have had a family member who suffered from a particular problem that required tremendous sacrifice on the part of the family. When the family finds out there are no support groups or services to help them, they may decide to form an organization to help others who are also in need. What starts out as a learning process for family survival becomes the beginning of a new career. There are probably success stories of this kind right in your community.

I can remember visiting one such organization where the person giving leadership was a survivor of her own family's tragedy and was now using her new-found skills and knowledge to help others. It did not take long to realize that the knowledge she had fell far short of what was by then available on a large scale in most communities. She was a very emotion-centered nurturing person, and as I continued to evaluate her small staff and volunteers, I found that they were nearly clones of the founder. Each one was poorly prepared but all were emotionally committed to one another. None of them had sufficient administrative knowledge or experience, and they had little interest in such things.

I had been asked to tell them how to get organized and secure the necessary funds for expanding their services. What I found was resistance to any real improvement or restructuring. They were not nearly as committed to meeting the requirements of their clients and constituents as they were to fulfilling their own personality needs through social action. Although their statements of purpose and individual testimonies were flowered with declarations of service to their community and the like, it was very clear that what they were gaining in their work together was more important to them personally than what their clients would receive through organizational movement. That is the reality in some nonprofits, and I knew from experience that those people would cause an improvement process to fail. They liked things the way they were and it was their choice to maintain the status quo.

You may be a nonprofit leader who has realized that the place where you labor has attracted a group of people who have exhibited a greater interest in their own personal agenda than in the requirements of the mission. Since nonprofits tend to have a more democratic nature than the typical for-profit, you could find yourself outnumbered and outvoted when it comes to the subject of improvement. Whether the problem is the minority mentality or some other form of resistance, it is possible that, like the group just described, your group will be most happy to be left alone. In such cases, I would remind you of two things. The marketplace is a ripe plum for those who want to do good and do it right, and quality people will attract quality people.

Chapter Review

The "psychology of quality" is a term used to describe the process of finding and eliminating the emotional and cognitive obstacles to improvement. These obstacles may not be easy to see because we have carried them with us for years unaware of their consequences. They are often submerged in the myth and mystique of our culture.

Management traditions include the things we learn directly and indirectly about management. They have a great impact on our selection of business systems and initiatives, language, methods, and enterprises. A manager's incorrect belief that it is against the law for a nonprofit organization to be profitable can create a distinctive resistance to some concepts of good business practice, profitability, and quality management. *List some of the management traditions in your area of work that have been brought into question as you have read through this book.*

Philosophical goodness can present one of the most subtle obstacles to quality management. When the goodness of a mission is overemphasized, the disciplines necessary to organize and deliver services of the highest quality may be difficult to achieve. Acts of goodness are common supporting fibers in a nonprofit work. But their presence in your behavior is no assurance that anything else you do is appropriate, honest, or effective. Goodness is difficult to measure, and improving on goodness or expressing more goodness than someone else might prove to be futile. To rise above the rest, you need to improve the quality of the good things you do. *Write down some aspects of your work that example goodness. To demonstrate how difficult it is to improve on goodness, try to describe the process of goodness.*

Social mystique is a function of goodness. It is an aura surrounding the activities of nonprofit work that causes people to believe in the value of what we do. To enjoy the benefits of social mystique, the nonprofit worker need not be especially efficient, organized, or effective at his or her work as long as it is perceived by others that they are trying to do good. Some individuals and organizations exist primarily on the basis of their ability to market social mystique. When that is the case, it is difficult to gain a commitment to quality management. *List some of the benefits of social mystique that your organization has received.*

The minority mentality is a label ascribed to certain mindsets and behavioral expressions that commonly surface among nonprofit minorities. It can represent a complex system of personal insecurities and individual personality needs, as well as certain culturally based obstacles. The minority mentality causes nonprofit organizations to: focus so much on society's awareness of their minority status that little or nothing is actually accomplished on behalf of its constituents; rely more on saying than doing; lose sight of stewardship responsibilities; fail to capitalize on opportunities for enterprise; sow and reap meaningless rhetoric; have unreasonable expectations of society; be oblivious to the fact that nearly all of us fit into some minority group with special needs. These attributes and behaviors can dramatically limit an organization's ability to function according to specific mission requirements. *Can you see any of these in your organization? If so, list them.*

Many people have pursued the cause of inappropriate behaviors and attitudes in their lives only to find that the behavior did not exist prior to an incident of personal rejection. Our greatest vulnerabilities exist with the special friend, teacher, or authority who has the ability to crush our tender souls.

Sometimes our environment repeatedly produces a feeling of rejection, and our styles of behavior are so commonly developed within our minority community that we not only fail to recognize them but also have them reinforced and supported by others suffering the same pain. Some of those behaviors include: negative, defeatist, or arrogantly superior attitudes; inordinate prejudice; the compulsive pursuit of a selfish agenda; paranoia about others' perceptions of who we are; inordinate anger; compulsive needs for self-gratification and recognition; well-known and established "secret slang" used within the community; a distinct melody to our language in the form of a musical intonation or the consistent presence of a theme for rhetoric; whining and preaching that support rhetoric; the use of manipulation, guilt, and accusation; and combinations of one or more of these descriptions. *List some of the attitudes, language, or behaviors in your own life or organization that need healing. Identify the incidents of rejection in your life and forgive the individuals involved.*

The public's reactions to the minority mentality is commonly predictable: more rejection. The minority mentality also acts as a social magnet and — like traditional thinking, goodness, and social mystique — attracts people who have the same viewpoint. The leader who recognizes the presence of some of these factors and takes on the responsibility for change must demonstrate improvement through his or her personal example before broadening efforts to the organization. *What are the social magnets in your organization? Which ones, if any, could cause problems in implementing quality management?*

7

Quality Management: A Lifestyle for the Long Run

Personal values, ethics, integrity, and self-discipline form the unseen government in all social systems.

Management Values

Quality management is best understood as a lifestyle of managing processes for quality. It is a management style for the long run that is rooted in individual and corporate values. Our individual standards for appropriate behavior, values, ethics, and morality will eventually manifest themselves in our management style. If we take short cuts in our personal lives, our management style will follow. If we hold to high standards of integrity and ethics in our private lives, they will also become part of our corporate managerial behaviors. This intermingling of individual and corporate values is particularly evident when we compare the immediate versus the long-term consequences of our decisions.

I have a friend who had been administering in a nonprofit environment for many years with above-average success. He told me about how he had decided to return to a learning structure provided by a local university and the discoveries he had made while attending classes. To his surprise, he had learned that the methods he had been depending on for success were largely incomplete. They were not dramatically wrong in most cases, but he had not been functioning anywhere near the levels of success that could be achieved with the new information he had acquired. What he had learned was significantly altering his personal opinions and management values, especially when he confronted the ethical nature of his discoveries. He had for many years defended his training and resource manageent methods on the basis of his good intentions and ethical values. After learning some new methods and techniques, he realized that he could not only more fully conform to his client's requirements but could also improve others' perceptions of his ethics.

Individual and corporate values are under siege in today's society. More than ever, routine interactions with various segments of our community turn out to be experiences in which our values are challenged and our methods questioned. The difficulty lies in knowing when to adopt or reject new ideas. Most of us find criticism to be a two-edged sword of good and bad, even at its best. Sometimes even the most constructive criticism is more than we can bear. Past rejections have a way of hardening a person's defenses to the point where even helpful messages cannot penetrate. This resistance can sometimes be so obvious that a person's integrity is brought under suspicion by observers who are unaware of his or her personal history.

Corporate integrity is fundamentally dependent on expressions of individual integrity. How a nonprofit organization is perceived by its constituents has a lot to do with the cumulative expressions of the individual values and behaviors of its staff. Because of this interdependence, the nonprofit leader must always be willing to subject his or her personal integrity and values to the test of criticism. The goals, systems, and methods of an organization will not be considered sacred and untouchable by a person who has routinely had his or her choices examined.

The process of quality improvement will bring every value and standard under scrutiny, beginning with the leadership life of the manager. It will also bring each trustee, staff member, and volunteer into the place of self-examination by creating an environment where nothing is as valuable as reality. Out of those experiences will come the corporate expressions of integrity that galvanize public support.

Community Standards

Communities have a tendency to establish their own standards for behavior. Whether it is done formally through law or informally through peer pressure, it is usually well known. Each member of a community is aware of what is generally or specifically expected in behavior, largely on the basis of the history of the particular community. The United States Supreme Court has recognized this dynamic in many of its decisions, noting that the same law or standard can be interpreted and enforced quite differently in two communities.

We can encounter conflict with our community when our standards of behavior are lower than the established norms. When that happens, our peers express their disfavor in ways that have become accepted by the group as appropriate. The person or organization pursuing quality improvement will also find that exceeding community standards can be perceived negatively. Instead of being commended for excellence, it is entirely possible that the quality leader will be subjected to unwarranted suspicion and judgment. The truth is that communities do not approve of behaviors less than or greater than their own without some questioning.

A young man I know made it a practice to set his own performance standards a little higher than what was expected of him by his superiors. Consequently, he never worried about doing too little or slacking off on the job. Occasionally his well-reasoned efforts produced superior performances that made some of his peers nervous. His experience in sales is a good example. At one company he was consistently the top producer. He had set his goals for learning the product a little higher than was expected of him. He practiced sales scenarios and planned for contingencies with regularity. He wanted to make sales and was convinced that doing the best job for his clients was the way to do it. As he looked back at those experiences, he was the best prepared, most dedicated salesperson in his division. The results were obvious, but not necessarily appreciated by everyone doing the same job.

When he entered the nonprofit world, he was looking forward to working among people who believed in doing good and doing it well. Surely people who were sacrificing so much for high ideals would appreciate performing to high standards. He was surprised to find the same suspicious reactions among some of his nonprofit peers as he had found in his previous for-profit experiences. He regularly received "encouragement" to ease off and not take the mission so seriously. He figured that if he believed enough in the ideals of the mission to make the financial and social sacrifices required in order to serve, that it was reasonable to hold to very high standards of performance.

When I began to evaluate the reactions of his nonprofit peers, I found them to be similar to others I had observed in two important ways. First, the people who were the most uncomfortable with high standards of performance were either untrained or poorly trained to do their jobs. Second, the value people placed on excellence was equal to their commitment to grow and learn. Those with very high standards for excellence were pursuing knowledge and discipline to improve their capabilities. Others who had adjusted their performance standards down to their current capabilities were unhappy to have the status quo disturbed.

In ancient times standards in the community were set by the most experienced and revered persons who had established credibility in their work. Whether those persons were called masters, elders, or the like, the basis for their recognition was established through practice and improvement over time. Their skill, knowledge, and maturity were respected and valued by the community and became the goal most desired by every individual.

Today, in both the for-profit and nonprofit worlds, setting a personal standard to become an elder or master at your work can create some friction in your community. While you are busy raising your level of performance and improving your capabilities, others may find it more pleasing to redefine and lower the standards. Don't worry. In your hearts, you will both know the difference.

Philanthropic Influence

Professional grantmakers are the managers of the profits generated by capitalism, competition, and innovation. As such, you might expect them to exhibit many of the same values as their benefactors in the grantmaking process. Surprisingly, it is very common, especially when the benefactor who endowed the foundation is deceased, to find grantmakers taking a largely ambivalent and sometimes reactive position to enterprise.

The mission of some of the larger private foundations is to influence intellectual and social systems through the funding of research. Studies of our educational and welfare systems that were funded by major private foundations have contributed greatly to the development of our current standards for public education, social justice, and political ethics. Although, in some cases, their investments have yielded significant improvements in the public attitude toward discrimination and human rights issues, an interesting pattern emerges as you survey the research and publication agenda of grantmaking organizations. You will find that the politically and socially conservative funds have produced research supporting their issue perspectives, and the liberal funds have done the same.

It is very clear that in social research some grantmakers' understanding of innovation is to create new ways to promote their own special interests and viewpoints. The idea of pursuing research for the common good has become little more than polite rhetoric. Because this mind-set exists in philanthropy, some of what grantmakers do has deteriorated into the art of giving to fulfill their private agenda. Of course, there are foundations and individual philanthropists large and small who are funding creative and enterprising work across the land. In numbers they are probably larger than the ones I have just described, but in political power and influence, a minority of foundations with the dollars to finance its expressions have produced some impressive results.

The person pursuing quality should be aware that although grantmakers may use the words "leveraged," "strategic," and "enterprise" in their business vocabulary, these words might not mean what that person thinks they should. Many foundation executives lack hands-on experience in the for-profit or nonprofit world. Some have been elevated to leadership from bureaucratic or academic environments with strong political or social agendas and little or no understanding of enterprise. Even so, quality is nearly irresistible to grantmakers, no matter what their political or social orientation. Although a favorable response requires that your work be within the scope of their grantmaking guidelines, you might be surprised at how far they will stretch to invest in a service of high quality.

Enterprising nonprofits are the most efficient forms of philanthropy. For-profit entrepreneurs who create profits or surpluses must then identify their areas of interest for philanthropy. Whether they choose to create a foundation, give through established grantmaking organizations, or donate directly to nonprofits, an additional process for investment must be supported. This includes applications and other communications and decision-making processes that consume energy and resources. The profits of the nonprofit entrepreneur flow directly into well-established service delivery systems. When those services are carefully managed to meet the requirements of society, effectively and efficiently the ultimate in doing good is achieved.

Professional Services

At some time during the life of a nonprofit organization, it will probably be necessary to hire outside professional help. Whether it is a lawyer to help you with your charter, an accountant to organize your books, or some other specialized consultant, their assistance can greatly influence the success of your organization.

Some managers tell me that they would like to have some specialized professional help but cannot afford the fee. I can understand how a developing nonprofit might not have cash in its budget for professional services and, frankly, sometimes a less experienced volunteer may have more than enough capability to help. Money should not be wasted in hiring professional services that are not needed. However, the services of a consultant who is going to solve a problem that is beyond the capabilities of the organization can be very inexpensive when measured against the cost of doing things wrong.

A nonprofit organization I have helped had decided that it was going to build a new facility for its services and had obtained letters of support from local and county governments and other community leaders. Nearly everywhere it turned, it was receiving very positive responses to the concept of a new facility. The need had been clearly demonstrated and land had been donated upon which to build. The only thing left to do was to begin a fund-raising drive for the several million dollars needed for the project. A kickoff luncheon was planned and the pledge cards were being printed.

I was invited to a board of directors meeting to discuss some of the plans for hiring an executive director to manage the greatly expanded programs the new facility would support. During one of these discussions, I asked one of the participants how much money a particularly public letter of support represented. She answered that money had not been discussed but she was sure the person could be depended on to make a pledge. This piqued my interest, so I chose another letter writer and asked the same question. Again, I received a response of assumption about the person's ability and intentions. I had discovered a potentially fatal flaw in their planning. No one had undertaken the responsibility to discuss with these "supporters" what they and/or their organization would be able to pledge to the program. So, even though the organization had strong rhetoric to support its expansion plans, the strength of the financial base was in doubt. We discussed the types of questions that should be asked of these special friends and how to go about converting the flow of words into dollars. We discovered that only one or two of the board members had any experience in fund-raising, and that was limited.

This organization was about to undertake a major fund-raising program and was already planning the expenditure of additional dollars for staff before thoroughtly analyzing its support base to determine the viability of the project. If someone within the ranks had had the time and ability to perform the research, I would have recommended it, but it was now time to hire an expert.

For the price of a part-time secretary, the organization engaged a professional fund-raiser who saved it from disaster. In his first report, he detailed the responses of the supporters

who had been encouraging the organization to move forward
in its project. His studies produced solid management information that the project would not be supported financially by these
very same people. The cost of the kickoff luncheon alone would
have been more than he was paid for his services, and the organization also avoided the loss of other development costs and
community favor. Eventually he was able to design a campaign
that proved to be successful. This is clearly a case where quality was free. What was spent doing things right was considerably less than what would have been spent failing.

Human Resources

The human resources available to a nonprofit organization are its most valuable assets, as well as being among the most
difficult to assess. Whether the relationship is external through
friends and consultants or internal from board members, staff,
and volunteers, the flow of information through people is critical to the operation of any enterprise. Because of the great need
for advice that we all face in nonprofit work, we sometimes find
ourselves with the problem of not knowing whom to ask and when.

Let us begin with the "whom to ask" part of this two-part
and interrelated process. Managers generally ask people within
their reach for information upon which to make process decisions. This means that staff members provide the most constant
source of input for the manager because they are within reach
on the job. When it comes to knowledge about a process, the
people running the process are the most valuable source of information. However, when the decision is about the person running a process, where do you go? The routine usually involves
confidential interviews with other staff or board members, but
the question lurking in the back of the mind of every manager
at these times is, "How reliable is this information?" You are
making decisions upon, or at the very least being influenced
by, the judgment of other people. How can you be sure that
the advice you receive is good advice? The truth is, you cannot
be sure. A lot will depend on your own experience and insight
and your ability to separate the precious from the worthless.

You can, however, increase the probability of receiving reliable input by carefully selecting your human resources in advance of the need for counsel.

The time to begin evaluating the probable reliability of human resources is prior to their insertion into your internal structure. Unreasonable assumptions about a person's value to your organization which are made prior to their becoming active in your processes will almost always rise up to haunt you, especially at the time of crisis. You can probably remember a person you selected whom you knowingly failed to ask key questions because of some assumption you were making about his or her talent, experience, or character. After you made the selection, certain behaviors may have surfaced that caused you to think you should have asked that key question during the initial interviews. Then comes the critical time of need and you are in turmoil about the reliability of that person's performance. Choosing whom to trust is at the heart of any manager's agenda. No one can be sure every time but some prudent steps can help.

First, before you select a board or staff member, volunteer or consultant, take the time to explain thoroughly your mission and the requirements for which you are asking them to share responsibility. Let them ask questions and be sure they have obtained an understanding of the requirements.

Second, ask them about their "goals" in life and how they fit into your agenda. Do not hesitate to probe deeply into this sacred territory.

Third, find out about their experience, education, and professional discipline. An application or résumé will serve as a good guide for your conversation, even for a volunteer. Persons interested in or desiring to help your mission are valuable only if they have the capability to do so. By questioning them in specific areas according to your needs, you can eliminate choices that will require extensive training or support you may not be able to provide.

Fourth, check out their references. Obtain permission from the interviewees to ask their references about their relationship, work history, integrity, and so on. Do not chicken out. It will cost you dearly if you fail to follow through.

Finally, if all of these check out positively, evaluate your personal compatibility with the individual. Compatibility is the last checkpoint. When it is the first checkpoint, you may have a tendency to overlook things you will later regret.

Setting reliable standards for selection will not guarantee anyone's performance, but it will eliminate some of the questions that will be too late to ask "when" you need reliable counsel.

Teaching and Training

Holding to high standards as you move into a process will prevent errors that can occur once it is established. This is particularly true when it comes to the placement of human resources within an organization. Managers who take the time to prepare their people to serve effectively are spending time that can be allocated in advance. Errors have a way of spending time and energy for you when you are least able to spare them, so preventative training is very inexpensive time to spend.

Teaching people to do things right is the place to begin any orientation process. Well before you tell them what you expect of them on the job, you should set the stage for training by teaching them about quality management. When people understand that you will expect them to learn the requirements of their work and fulfill them, you will have begun a process within them that will help them to fit comfortably into your organization. As you explain prevention, the standard of zero defects, and the costs of doing things wrong, you will also gain a better student.

Specialized training should be designed for every person in the organization, including board members and volunteers. The principles of quality management should be reinforced in each phase of training, with generous opportunities given to the trainees to talk about their questions and concerns. Although the following is not a blueprint, there are five phases of training that have proven very useful to me over the years.

- *Phase one:* tell them. This includes lectures, discussions, reading assignments, and the use of audio and video aids. In this phase, you are transmitting information to the trainee. It is entirely appropriate to check to see if the information is being retained. This can be accomplished formally or informally through oral or written methods.

- *Phase two:* show them. Actually do what it is you will expect of them and let them watch and ask questions as you do it. In some cases, it will be more reasonable for the trainee to write questions down and ask them later. Again, be sure that there is generous time for interaction and that important quality management principles are reemphasized.

- *Phase three:* help them. This time you watch them perform the task and make mental notes of improvements that you can emphasize once they have completed one cycle of the task. Be ready to help at any time but give them the freedom to fail without fear. Repeat the cycle several times until they begin to relax and perform routinely.

- *Phase four:* partner them. This is *not* on-the-job training. Place them under the leadership of one of their peers in the organization. This person will take your place in helping them. Have the peers share responsibility with the trainee, alternately doing and then watching. Encourage the trainees to discuss their viewpoints about quality and to take time to review the organization's philosophy. Stop by to say hello and provide encouragement but do not teach or train during the visits—just observe.

- *Phase five:* empower them. After you have received a positive report from their peer, meet with them again to discuss the entire training program. This should be done in a relaxed and informal atmosphere. By this time, the trainee should have the ability to ask penetrating questions about the process and provide excellent feedback about what has been learned. You may also pick up tips on how to improve your training process. Finish your interview by assigning specific responsibilities and empowering the trainee to perform.

The trainer should always be ready to repeat a phase so that the trainee is confidently in control of the information and actions required. In some cases, it will become clear that the trainee is not going to be able to perform effectively. Do not hesitate to reassign the trainee to another training process or to allow him or her to exit the organization with grace. This is particularly important with volunteers.

The manager who learns to take these investments of his or her time seriously will also come to appreciate the absence of chaos in routine operations. As has been said before, you can pay me now or you can pay me later.

Team Building

When we talk of improving processes and services, the emphasis is on fulfilling the requirements of the mission. Every part of an organization must pull together for the mission to be consistently performed. That oneness of purpose is often referred to as unity. Traditional concepts of unity include such factors as loyalty, sacrifice, and being of one mind. When this occurs naturally as a group of people respond individually in like manner toward a common objective, the result is called a team.

Being part of a team can be one of life's special satisfactions. A team laboring well together will accomplish more work than the same number of individuals working independently. This dynamic is called synergism and when it exists, one and one are greater than two. It is a great experience to be part of a cohesive and well-trained team of coworkers. The sense of belonging and working together creates relationships that will last long after the objectives are obtained.

Modern industry has recognized the benefits of team building and has devised various ways of encouraging it. The quality circle and other such methods of team building have had dramatic effects on productivity and morale. When people are given the opportunity to contribute to leadership and are allowed to hold themselves accountable to standards they have helped establish, they begin to work as if they own the process. This feeling of ownership causes them to increase their attentiveness and caring. The resulting work behaviors add to the team member's sense of well-being and increase the value of work life.

One of the important factors that makes team members

feel secure is recognition by the group that the individual well-being of the team members is more important than the team objective. In other words, a team would never sacrifice the well-being of a teammate in order to reach a team goal. In fact, one team member would hold another member back from unreasonable personal sacrifices. A team desires to sacrifice equally in an effort, even though sometimes one or more members of the team may demonstrate leadership in this area.

Team building is an art more than a science. Although there are identifiable attributes to a team, the most anyone can do is create the potential. There are people with outstanding charisma that have the ability to lead a group of people more effectively than others. However, most managers can achieve the basis for synergism by following a few simple principles.

If we select and train people with well-established and consistently implemented guidelines, we greatly increase the potential for team building. Beyond that, a common objective, a commitment to quality, a sincere conern for the team members, and a dedicated leader can cause wonderful things to happen. When these factors are not present, things can occur that are not so pleasant.

In the nonprofit world, it is not uncommon to find a zealous and charismatic person giving leadership to a band of excited and dedicated people ready to sacrifice unreasonably for the goodness of the mission. Group members' personalities are often accentuated by a need to belong and a willingness to release their personal rights. On the surface, this sounds to some like the basis for team building, although what occurs within the organization may not produce synergism, efficiency, or effectiveness.

Some organizations exist on human sacrifices. They are sacrifices of energy, relationships, finances, and personal value that the participants cannot afford but naively make for the greater good of the group's objective. I call this process "throughput."

Throughput is very simply the consumption of human assets, drawn from people who pass through an organization, to meet the organization's needs. When this occurs, the needs of the organization's clients are rarely met with any effectiveness because the organization consumes most of its resources in inefficiency. Throughput is a term used in manufacturing to describe how many resources travel through a process toward the destination of production. In this example, they are consumed within the process and the participants are usually not around long enough to declare the invalidity of it all.

Organizations existing on throughput have some common characteristics. They talk about a team effort but they have no standards for joining the team, little or no training, and an objective that is difficult to measure. The leader can be expected to keep the "team" hyped-up on promises and predictions of results that are just a tomorrow away and that rarely take place. The output of this process is measured in human loss instead of human gains, and the victims are left to wonder if they were the only ones who felt something was wrong.

When you set about building your team, you will invariably use some of the same words that the "throughput" organization uses. That will account for the strange reactions you may see in some of the individuals you are interviewing. They may have heard those words before. Keep this in mind and be sensitive to their need to talk through all of their fears. By answering their questions and being consistent in your own behaviors, you may all achieve your "team" goals.

Organizational Development

Organizations are like people. They grow and develop in their personality and capability through various stages of life. When we know what it is we want to accomplish with our organizational life, we can then decide what education and experience we will need. By comparing the requirements of our mission to the capabilities of our organization, we can map out a plan for improvement and growth that will carry us to the desired destination. It is very similar to the process that a young adult goes through in selecting and preparing for a career.

The early growth of a nonprofit organization from one stage of development to the next cannot be predicted with any more accuracy than that of a young child. Although potential can be assessed, what the organization will choose to do with that potential will be played out through the interaction of the best-laid plans and life's influences. However, as time and experience begin to have their effect, the predictability of outcomes can become more certain. The more choices a person or organization makes, the more predictable future choices become.

What makes quality management so helpful is that whether we are in the earliest stages of development or have moved into predictable patterns of achievement, the management of opportunities is guided by our perception of the requirements as they currently exist. As requirements and goals change, we can continue our momentum toward improvement. We can do this by assessing current opportunities against our best understanding of our organization's requirements. Then we can create the basis for deliberate growth by choosing the options that most closely fit.

Each stage of development should build on the successes of the previous stage. As people or organizations grow and mature, certain capabilities surface as evidence of what they have already accomplished. This information is critical in making choices about future growth.

A young woman who has selected the arts and has demonstrated capability over time and into adulthood is developing a momentum toward quality and achievement that can be augmented and nurtured. Although it is possible that she might suddenly switch her interest to the sciences, the probability of meeting the requirements of this new endeavor may be questionable. There are certainly people who have sucessfully achieved a radical retargeting of their lives, but for most individuals—and organizations—such a change would be statistically improbable.

Strategic planning is a process designed to identify your capabilities and to get you from where you are to where you want to be. It is a very helpful tool that can be used to foster organizational development. Strategic planning is much more than organizing your approach to choices. It requires being aware. It is not enough to organize choices into categories and options. The possible consequences of those choices must be fully evaluated and understood.

As part of overall organizational development and quality improvement, the strategic planning process is an exploration that allows you to fully integrate options, standards, and ethics into a doable plan. It is friendly to and sometimes synonymous with quality improvement in that everyone's requirements end up on the table for analysis.

When I am asked by the board of a nonprofit organization to help them design their strategic plan, I often find that their concept of what should happen is highly simplistic. They believe they will tell me where they are and where they want to go and I will tell them how to do it. I have tried many times to explain how strategic planning is a comprehensive process and have found that the best time to present that viewpoint is after the first hour or two of listening to a handful of board members discover how differently they see where they are. In fact, as they move through the strategic planning process, they will become aware of how far apart they are on a number of issues that supposedly were well established within their mission.

Obtaining everyone's input, including key staff members and volunteers, and placing it into a logical sequence of agreed-upon steps as a guideline for development, is only the first phase of strategic planning. Actions must be regularly evaluated according to the strategic plan, and as requirements change, the plan must change with them in a dynamic process of reevaluation. If our lifetime goals include moving into organizational adulthood and the mentoring of others, we must be prepared to discipline ourselves into mature growth and to plan carefully for tomorrow.

Using Reasonable Judgment

Laws enacted by government, and rules, creeds, and bylaws designed by organizations or associations, are all fulfilling a common purpose. They are presenting a standard for behavior on behalf of a community. A community's values, ethics, concepts of integrity, and expectations for self-discipline are expressed through laws and rules. These are used to hold individuals responsible for their behavior and to encourage them to act within the guidelines of the total community's reasonable judgment.

Laws are limited in their effectiveness in that they are only enforceable for acts of irresponsibility that can be seen and measured by the community. This judgment varies in that the measures are based on each community's concept of what is reasonable. Throughout the various laws of local, state, and federal governments, the measurement of "reasonableness" occurs repeatedly. Obviously, what is reasonable behavior for one group may vary greatly for another, but the more important issue may be what is unreasonable. This is never more evident than in our financial accountability.

A for-profit company is free to earn and spend its money as it desires. There are, however, limits on certain expenditures judged as unreasonable because the owner or employees of a company would benefit unfairly from its transactions. There are dozens of such limitations on what a for-profit company can do reasonably within the confines of its corporate operations, not to mention those that the stockholders may want to impose.

In a nonprofit organzization, many of the same standards for expenditures apply, again so that individuals do not unfairly or improperly benefit from their relationship. In addition, the responsibility to manage for the public good is involved. This means that salaries and expenses must meet the test of "reasonableness" for the work that is being accomplished. Again, reasonableness may depend on the cumulative judgment of the individuals in a community because, ultimately, social judgment by our peers and constituents will prevail. This takes place both formally through the imposition of law and informally through public reaction.

When a nonprofit wastes, misuses, or unreasonably spends the dollars at its disposal, it is often wasting someone else's money. The gifts and contributions received are considered to be part of a trust or stewardship relationship. Certainly, when a contributor makes such a gift, he or she formally gives up control of that asset as it becomes commingled with other public expressions of support. However, the organization will be held accountable informally by the constituents and formally by law for the proper stewardship of those assets.

These same public measures can be applied to other areas of management, including the types and quality of the services provided to the public. When there is a failure that results in personal injury or loss, the public has historically dealt generously and kindly with nonprofits because of their good works and limited resources. However, this public attitude is changing dramatically. Members of the legal profession now talk openly in seminars about the need to penetrate the legal and social umbrellas of nonprofits to hold them accountable for their actions. Their ability to prevail in a court of law will, in most cases, be dependent upon their ability to demonstrate that the nonprofit organization was not using reasonable judgment.

In these cases and others where social judgment will bear on a decision, the written records of an organization may serve as the best defense of reason and prudence. Those standards and requirements that should produce behaviors well within the rule of social judgment might also help to protect you from the appearance of operating without reasonable care or concern. Policy and procedure manuals, training materials, and detailed process requirements are the best evidence of intent when the reasonable expectations of a community are not achieved in a particular instance. Even the organization striving for improvement can occasionally fail to meet public expectations. A lot may depend on whether that failure is perceived as unreasonable.

The Whistle Blower

Nearly every industry can point to some individuals within its ranks who have demonstrated unreasonable behaviors in their transactions and have eventually become an example of what is wrong. The same applies to the nonprofit world. Within its various segments, there are always a few who are dazzling us with their footwork as they dodge and weave through the moral and social issues, fulfilling their own selfish agendas.

Hardly a year goes by without the report of a nonprofit organization found to be violating widely held moral, ethical, or financial standards. In fact, some nonprofit citizens have joined those in the for-profit world and government in what has become known as "whistle blowing." Instead of waiting for the behaviors of an individual or organization to become so bizarre that they can be observed and measured by the public, they take what is to them a moral and ethical stand against undiscovered misconduct. They provide the information that will bring formal and informal pressures on the violator. In some cases, these disclosures result in legal action, while in others, social pressure alone creates the initiative for change.

Becoming a whistle blower takes an enormous amount of courage, since the short-term consequences can mean personal rejection by associates, as well as loss of income. Although, in most cases, the wheels of justice eventually vindicate the honest and accurate whistle blower, the price paid in personal stress and discomfort can be enormous. The targets of a whistle blower can become so vile in their behavior or so deceived by their position of importance that they do not hesitate to manipulate whatever powers are necessary to silence oppostion.

Both the decision to become a whistle blower and the behaviors that might need to be exposed begin as matters of an individual's heart and conscience. In the case of the whistle blowers, there is a decision not to remain silent in the presence of obvious injustice, inequity, or a moral issue of consequence. By responding to their own conscience, they produce behaviors that force these issues to be confronted. In the case of the persons exposed, the behaviors began as a result of failing to obey their conscience. With each opportunity to violate their conscience, their behaviors became more overtly inappropriate and the inner "whistle" of their hearts more often silent.

There is little in the world quite as precious as a clear conscience and few things as pitiful as one who has lost it. The simple act of speaking truth from our hearts is pivotal in the structuring and development of our individual attitudes and behaviors. In most cases, this structuring is dynamic and is either moving toward a clear conscience or a lost one on a day-to-day basis. When we observe unusual acts of imprudence or misconduct, we often ask, "how does a person get that way?" One day as I pondered the predicament of a counselee's life, I asked myself the same question about her plight. The answer that suddenly came to me was, "one step at a time." A person can begin the road to moral and ethical decline with small and apparently insignificant acts only bordering on dishonesty. This can occur as simply as making the confident assertion that we can perform work that we are not adequately skilled, trained, or experienced to accomplish. This is certainly not limited to those holding positions within a nonprofit organization, but also applies to licensed or credentialed individuals who provide counsel or professional services.

Our conscience provides us with the guidance we need when we are moving counter to our moral or ethical standards. Entering the process of quality improvement will bring specific and measurable requirements into focus that will provide healthy opportunities to exercise and strengthen our conscience. After all, in its purest sense, the pursuit of quality is a matter of the heart.

Chapter Review

Quality management is best understood as a lifestyle of managing processes for quality. Our individual standards for appropriate behavior, values, ethics, and morality will eventually manifest themselves in our management style. The nonprofit leader must always be willing to subject his or her values to the test of criticism because the process of quality management will bring every value and standard under scrutiny, beginning with the leadership life of the manager. *List some of the personal values that you would like to see expressed through your organization's pursuit of quality management.*

The person or organization pursuing quality improvement may find that exceeding community standards is perceived negatively and causes them to be subjected to unwarranted suspicion or judgment. Communities do not approve of behaviors less than or greater than their own without some questioning. In ancient times community standards were set by the most experienced and revered persons who had established credibility in their work. Today, setting a personal standard to become a master at your work can create some friction. While you are busy raising your level of performance, others may find it more pleasing to redefine and lower standards. Do not worry. In your hearts, you both will know the difference, and contributors definitely will take notice.

Professional grantmakers are the managers of the profits generated by capitalism, competition, and innovation. Even so, some grantmakers take an ambivalent or reactive position to enterprise. This may be because many foundation executives lack hands-on experience in either the for-profit or nonprofit world. Some have been elevated to leadership from bureaucratic or academic environments with strong political or social agendas and little or no understanding of enterprise. However, when your work is within the scope of a foundation's grantmaking guidelines, you will be excited to see that quality is nearly irresistible to these same people. Enterprising nonprofits are the most efficient forms of philanthropy. When the profits of the nonprofit entrepreneur flow directly into well-established, effective, and efficient service delivery systems, the ultimate in doing good is achieved.

At some time during the life of a nonprofit organization, it will probably be necessary to hire outside professional help. Whether this help is a lawyer, accountant, or some other specialized consultant, their assistance can greatly influence your success. Instead of paying for services, sometimes a less experienced volunteer can perform the needed service. However, the services of a professional in solving a problem beyond the capabilities of an organization can be very inexpensive compared to the cost of doing things wrong. *Professionals and volunteers can fail to deliver as promised because they did not fully understand the requirements. Can you think of a time that happened? Describe the price of nonconformance.*

Whether you are hiring professionals or recruiting staff and volunteers, the human resources of an organization are its most valuable asset. Choosing people properly is critical. This is particularly evident when you are in crisis and feel uncertain about the capabilities or reliability of the people in your organization. Establishing standards for all interviews and training will help.

For Interviews:

- First, thoroughly explain your mission and its requirements. Ask questions to make sure the interviewee understands.
- Second, ask questions to find out how the person's goals fit into your agenda.
- Third, find out about his or her experience, education, and/or professional discipline.
- Fourth, talk to his or her references. Ask about his or her relationship, work history, integrity, and so on.
- Finally, if all these check out positively, then evaluate your personal compatibility.

In training you should begin by teaching about quality management and explaining your commitment to fulfilling requirements. Then you can tell the trainees what you expect of them on the job and begin their training. As as example here are five phases of training:

- *Phase one:* tell them what you want through lectures, discussion, reading assignments.
- *Phase two:* show them what you want by actually doing the job and letting them watch.
- *Phase three:* help them by watching them perform the task and standing by for questions and support.
- *Phase four:* partner them with another worker who will take your place in helping them.
- *Phase five:* empower them when you and their coworker are satisfied they are ready to work alone.

The failure to follow a well-planned approach to human resource issues can result in great losses. *From your own experiences, describe the price of nonconformance in a situation where that happened.*

Being part of a team laboring together to fulfill an organization's mission requirements can be one of life's special satisfactions. When we select and train people using well-established and consistently implemented guidelines, we greatly increase the potential for team building. Beyond that, a common objective, a commitment to quality, a sincere concern for team members, and a dedicated leader can create wonderful results. As organizations grow and develop, a team of dedicated workers can multiply the ability to plan strategically and take advantage of opportunities for growth. It can also help to hold an organization accountable to reasonable judgments that will maintain a clear management conscience. *What are some of the ways you plan to improve your organization's teamwork?*

8

The Quality Crusade:
A Strategy
for Implementing Change

Where there are words alone, even though the people understand, there will be no change.

—King Solomon
Proverbs 29:19

Quality Leadership

It is interesting to note that when especially disciplined and talented people are honored for their contributions to society, they invariably seem to mention someone who taught them a special principle to live by. Many times that principle has something to do with growing and learning as a person. Whether it is sports, music, the arts or sciences, our potential to improve is greatly enhanced when we have a desire to learn, no matter what abilities we start out with.

My dad coached youth baseball as a hobby and I occasionally attended practices and games to watch his teams. His teams were always very competitive and usually won their district or state title in their age group. Opposing coaches would lament that my dad ended up with all the good players or had some advantage at the annual tryouts. He did have an advantage. While the other coaches were looking only for the better

150

athletes or bigger and stronger boys, Dad was looking for those who demonstrated an interest in learning about baseball.

One of the first things he would tell all his players was that they were going to have fun playing baseball. Practice was lively but emphasized the fundamentals. The team would regularly sit on the ground around Dad and listen to baseball philosophy. While different players were practicing drills he had taught them, he might have all the outfielders or pitchers together in one corner of the field teaching them the special whys and hows of their positions. Those who needed special one-on-one attention got it as well. It took just a few practices for these average boys to start looking and acting above average when they were on a baseball diamond.

The players on these teams were always eager and pliable students because they had learned the joy of improvement. Every lecture, drill, and exercise was causing them to improve individually and as a team, and it did not take long for them to love being taught. They understood that everyone who wants to learn and improve can be a winner.

The quality leader must be able to kindle the fire of learning in those people he or she wants to lead into quality improvement. A group of people who are committed to their mission and dedicated to learning how to improve what they are doing can become a team that causes the other coaches to feel envy and the crowd to roar its approval.

A Cultural Challenge

When you review the subjects we have discussed in this book, it is easy to see that the process of bringing people together in a nonprofit environment to learn new concepts and improve what they are doing will take some premeditation. A "hooray" meeting may take place occasionally during the process of improvement, but obtaining a permanent cultural change is a far greater challenge than can be met by cheerleading. For quality improvement to take place, your people must be unified in their purpose and speaking the same language. That means you will need to know them well enough to prescribe the proper sequence of learning events needed to kindle their interest and enable them to understand and use the language of quality.

Examples abound of what can be accomplished when people unite in a common purpose. One of my favorites is found in the Book of Genesis, chapter 11. The ancient account states that at that time all the people on earth used the same language. On this occasion, the people had decided to build a city with a tower whose top would reach into heaven, and had set about their task. The Lord came down to see the city and the tower that the people were building and made this astonishing assessment: "Behold they are one people and they all have the same language. Nothing which they purpose to do will be impossible for them" (Gen. 11:6, New American Standard Version).

Their purposes were contrary to the purposes of God so he halted their progress by confusing their language so that they could not understand one another's speech. They stopped building the tower, and it was never completed as planned. The city was named Babel, which is the Hebrew word for confuse. This is an excellent example of what can happen when a group of people are not speaking the same language. No matter how much they have accomplished in the past and no matter how hard they try in the future, they cannot fulfill their purposes. But, when they speak the same words — that is, are of a like mind — all things are possible for them.

Establishing an awareness of and commitment to quality is not something you will want to rush into without careful and thoughtful study of the strategy that will work best in your organizational culture. Consideration must be given to informal structures and politics as well as the organization's established lines of authority. You will want to find and enlist true believers in your quality crusade and build a subculture that will magnify the lure of quality. Educational formats and training resources must also be considered along with the individual differences of people.

First and foremost, you must solidly obtain and display the benefits of quality in your own life. Achieving quality experiences will be relatively easy if you focus your efforts on self-improvement before you move to bring change to your organization. Keep records of your personal reactions to applying the quality principles. It will help to have a notebook handy to chronicle the questions, ideas, and comments you will have as you grow in quality awareness. You can also use the Chapter Review and Work-Study questions at the end of each chapter to reevaluate your mastery of the subject and to generate entries for your notebook.

Quality improvement is a subject that can bring you into exciting and productive conversation with your constituents. It must never be assumed, though, that you are speaking the same language and are in agreement. When you have had the opportunity to comprehend fully what you personally believe, you will be prepared to ask the questions that will test the understanding of your constituents. As these informal interactions take place, you will become more knowledgeable of the educational initiatives that will be needed to bring your nonprofit culture to an understanding of the language of quality.

Start in Your Garage

The quality crusade is one that requires a tremendous amount of thought and introspection on the part of the nonprofit manager. A successful crusade will have plenty of challenges waiting for the enthusiastic convert. To avoid causing unnecessary conflict because of misdirected zeal, I would encourage you to take your new-found revelation into the dark recesses of your garage before you spring it on the rest of your world.

Test your own commitment to quality improvement by using your energy to bring the maintenance of your car, lawn mower, and paintbrushes into conformance with the household's requirements. It will be good practice for you and the surprises and failures will be valuable experiences. They will also be hidden away in your garage out of sight. Once you have brought your garage under control, start through the other subsystems that make your house a home. Move slowly and take your time so that you can fully experience the discipline of pursuing quality.

Target your initial improvement crusade at your own life and personality. Then work with family and friends outside the workplace. Let it simmer and mature in you before you allow coworkers to know why your work results are improving. Whether you are at the top of your organization or a new volunteer, you must prove to yourself that you can manage for quality before the message will have a lasting effect on others.

Many people fail to understand that having all the right ingredients is not enough to be able to make the brew. Mixing the right ingredients in the wrong sequence can produce explosive and very destructive experiences. Likewise, careful thought should be given to what sequence of learning events must take place within our nonprofit environment even after we have proven ourselves at home and on the job. Premature and unplanned crusades can produce a useless and tasteless mix of initiatives that do no harm *and* no good. Although you may survive such an incident, the probability is that you will decrease the receptivity of your audience.

Planning a Strategy

To bring quality improvement to the forefront of your nonprofit culture, you will need a definite strategy for introducing the concepts and values of quality improvement. An effective strategy will convert your mission and objectives into performance and results.

The leadership of your organization must be convinced of the value of quality management for it to be introduced permanently into your culture. They have the authority and control of existing processes. So whether you are *a* manager, *the* manager, or someone down in the stack, you must create a plan to obtain the total commitment of top management. That plan would logically begin in your own garage. Later, if you are *the* manager, you would want to begin sharing with the members of your board of directors and fellow managers in a deliberate person-by-person approach. Take your time and teach them, building each person to the point of commitment.

As you begin to do your precinct work and spread seeds of thought in your fellow managers, you can also begin doing the research you will need to design the sequence of events that will follow once your management is committed to quality improvement. A strategy that works is always dependent on solid intelligence gathering. You must listen carefully to the words of your staff, volunteers, and clients and gain understanding of their attitudes and language. Keep a list of the words you know will have to be reconciled in their meaning and continue gathering information about your organization as you grow personally in quality awareness.

If you are a staff member or volunteer, your path may be longer but your strategy will initiate in the same manner. Start in your garage first, and so on. Then, by treating your superior as a customer, win his or her confidence and support by meeting the requirements for your performance in an extraordinary fashion. Build a reputation for personal quality and wait for your superior to ask you about your philosophy and standards. When your big opportunity comes, the ability to explain calmly the benefits and applications of quality improvement that you have experienced will go a long way toward piquing the interest of superiors.

Informal Structures and Politics

As you continue your personal growth, begin to make a list of the most influential people in your organization. A good method would be to use what some people call a ladder. At the country club, a tennis ladder is the pecking order of influence. Start out by listing the names in a column according to actual authority. Next to each name list the day-to-day results of one person's influence over another.

There may be four people of equal authority who hold essentially the same position in the organization. You might start by listing them alphabetically. Then watch daily to see which of them influences the others the most, the next most, and so on. Also be aware of who of the four has the most influence with his or her superior and why. List them in descending order of influence. If number three consistently influences number two, switch their positions on the ladder. The influence ladder will help you keep track of the informal structures and politics of your organization. It would not be unusual in a nonprofit environment to find that a volunteer who is lowest in the actual organizational chart may have more real influence with the top managers than anyone else. It is essential that you be aware of these informal dynamics. Remember, you will probably have more than one person of influence to convince, and maybe several from various levels of organizational authority.

To be worthwhile, this research cannot be done casually or occasionally. To have confidence in your research, you must be on the scene of routine operations within your organization and obtain enough repetitions of your data so that you can be sure they are correct. Your research will require an emphasis on listening. Talking about quality prematurely can expose your research intent and close down the spontaneity of your coworkers' comments. This is especially important when you begin to identify the political and social issues that provide strength to the various centers of influence. Be satisfied to listen and gather information patiently. Some issues that appear simple and uncomplicated on the surface may have deep roots in individual personalities or your organization's history. Take your time in uncovering these hot spots so you can be sure of the level of support or opposition to expect.

Find True Believers

Someone once said that the Peace Corps owed its success to its ability to engage the spiritually unemployed in useful work. There is a very real need among humankind to be helpful to others, and the nonprofit community has always been strongly dependent on that motive for the fulfillment of its mission. The will to make a personal sacrifice and the need for service are present in the life of nearly all nonprofit workers. They are rarely working for personal gain, although, as mentioned earlier, there are some who are driven by unusual personal needs and ambitions. It would logically follow that finding true believers in the nonprofit world should be an easy task. Actually, these factors make your task more difficult.

Those of us who work in the nonprofit world know that within the ranks of all the believers with whom we labor side by side, there are those who are spiritually *under*employed. They are not satisfied with the intensity of purpose within their organization or its capability in meeting the clients' needs. Because they feel organizational limitations, they are unable to find complete spiritual fulfillment in their work. They are sometimes irritating to the other believers who think things are "good enough." The spiritually underemployed should be identified in our research efforts because they are the true believers who will form the backbone of the quality improvement process.

Top-level managers who are spiritually underemployed should be brought into the seed-sowing process as soon as possible when you are their peer or superior. Their partnership can accelerate obtaining corporate commitment. If you are lower down the ladder, do not rush into a superior's office on a crusade. Stay back and wait for the recognition of your work or until an opportunity arises through natural relationships. Do not contrive or manipulate opportunities before their time.

Build a Subculture

If you allow the things we have discussed in this chapter to follow their own course, a quality improvement subculture will begin to form. As the concepts of quality improvement grow and mature in your own life and work, they will quite naturally produce seeds of interest in your coworkers. In those areas where you have authority, you can even venture out in leadership by teaching your subordinates about the quality concepts and using them in your work together.

One of the most vivid examples of the potential of a subculture was witnessed in 1989 as the effect of democratic principles on the young adult population of China took its course. We should not be surprised that the Chinese students in Tienanmen Square were quoting Thomas Jefferson. Many of their friends and fellow students had attended universities in the United States. Here they had been exposed not only to the history of great leaders such as Jefferson but also to a democratic system in their daily lives. These "democratized" students had told their friends about the values of democracy and had tapped into their society's individual desires for freedom. The results that Chinese exchange students who had lived in America could achieve would come as no surprise to the experienced crusader. When the model of the Statue of Liberty sprang up in Tienanmen Square, it was the result of seeds of democratic knowledge sown years before in the heart of a student hungry for freedom.

The tragedy of the Chinese massacre in Tienanmen Square is vivid enough on its own merits. Sadly, the subculture was growing vigorously in too small a segment of the society for the level of public demonstration to be successful. The subculture had not sufficiently gained support at the top of the political ladder. It was beginning to take root and had attained influence with a small minority of Chinese politicians, but as the events clearly demonstrated, the subculture was so new that the opposition easily prevailed. The potential for change in the overall population and the existence of a subculture are essential factors in the movement of a culture away from established norms. In an organization, without sufficient representation in top management, you will most likely fail.

The most difficult thing for a crusader to do is wait patiently for the subculture to grow and take root deeply. Sometimes our own enthusiasm blinds us to the very real resistance we will be facing and causes us to overestimate our strength. You will need grass-roots support throughout your organization, as well as a significant majority in top management. Of course, there are some organizations that will follow one leader's vision no matter what the cost, but the implementation of the concepts of quality improvement will require everyone to "own" the vision.

Seizing the Moment

I recall a recent movie in which a prep school teacher was continually exhorting his students to "seize the moment." It was interesting to see this dedicated teacher try to explain to his students how important today's "moment" can be. American culture encourages us to pursue our moment, but has drifted away from the importance of living out to the fullest each moment in life.

The quality crusader must obtain every possible benefit from the moments that occur during the development of the subculture. Goal-oriented persons who are driving toward the realignment of their culture must discipline themselves to savor fully the lessons and growth in each day. There will come a moment when the opportunity will exist to advance your cause within the top management of your organization. When it occurs, you will be very happy if you were patient and took time to prepare. The quiet confidence you will have obtained as you proved the quality principles in your own life and research will be your guarantee that quality improvement is well represented when *the* moment arrives.

Of course, what you say will be greatly influenced by your research and the experience you have had building a subculture, but it should include a definition of quality, a current assessment of your workplace, and a vision of what it could be. When the moment comes, you should know exactly which examples will capture your listener's attention. The objective of your presentation will be to gain an opportunity for comprehensive discussion of quality improvement. So plan to make your first moment short and to the point.

If you are the top manager in your organization, you can certainly be much more deliberate in your presentations to the board and key managers, but it will be very helpful for you to let the quality message grow in you before the crusade begins. In this process, everyone must own the quality concepts individually, as well as corporately. When the moment occurs, it will open the way for complete commitment of your organization's leadership to quality improvement. It will be well worth the wait.

Educating for Quality

Once you have obtained a commitment to quality improvement, you will want to teach every person in your organization the concepts and principles of quality. This process should begin with board members and top executives. Ultimately, every staff member and volunteer should receive a quality education. The process of educating your organization should be continuous, with considerations for educating new staff and volunteers, as well as reviewing quality concepts with the once-educated. The process of education has no end, only milestones.

This process cannot be accomplished in one day or weekend. You may want to begin with an organization-wide meeting to explain your organization's new commitment to quality and the requirement for everyone to participate in the educational activities. Then systematically, on a weekly basis, take one group of students at a time through the chapters in this book to establish them in quality thinking. Each group will take several weeks, with one or two hours per week in class, to discuss the new topic. When one group has completed the classes, start another group through until everyone has participated. The topics should follow the outline of the book with ample time to discuss the participants' questions and concerns.

- Chapter One: The Benefits. Give examples of how doing things wrong costs much more than doing things right. Focus on the marketability of quality and how conservation will provide lost-and-found dollars.
- Chapter Two: Quality Defined. Begin by focusing on requirements as the definition of what you want to accomplish. Define your client's requirements and practice making lists of requirements using processes at home and at work as examples.
- Chapter Three: Prevention and Cause. Discuss the difference between counting errors and preventing them from happening. Explain the importance of finding the cause of mistakes. Create a blameless environment.
- Chapter Four: The Quality Standard. Our commitment to high standards and our attitude toward errors will create the basis for performance. Discuss zero defects and eliminate the fears of perfection.

- Chapter Five: The Marketing Edge. Discuss the concepts of public entrepreneurship and marketing. Begin to identify the ways your organization can develop enterprising attitudes and activities. List your organization's marketable skills.
- Chapter Six: Eliminating Obstacles. This chapter may take twice as long to complete. Thoroughly discuss individual and corporate obstacles to quality and create an openness that will lead everyone to a commitment to improve.
- Chapter Seven: The Quality Lifestyle. This chapter will provide the basis for many weeks of discussion about the values that you will establish for various processes within your organization. It will foster a comprehensive look at requirements.
- Chapter Eight: The Quality Crusade. Encourage the participants to follow this simple path of improvement and to wait patiently for the educational process to complete its cycle through the staff and volunteers.

You may want to use the chapter reviews as a guide for class discussions. Remember, the first time through the organization is just the beginning. You will need to continue education to maintain an improvement awareness.

The Quality Improvement Committee

In the same way that obtaining quality in service processes requires the deliberate application of the principles of quality, the maintenance of a quality culture requires specific planning and action. Quality is pursued and quality awareness continues as a result of educational and training initiatives and the routine elimination of errors in client services.

Each organization will want to evaluate the educational and training activities that will be necessary to fully prepare every person entering the organization to operate in a quality culture. As board members, staff, and volunteers turn over, a prevention approach to quality education will be needed to avoid the dilution of the organization's commitment to quality. Also, communications procedures must be established to allow every worker the opportunity to focus the organization's attention on current problems as well as any recurring need for quality education. To make sure all of this happens, the requirements for the maintenance of a quality culture must be fashioned into a separate quality improvement process. The management of this process should rest in the hands of a specially organized quality improvement committee.

The quality improvement committee should include representation from the board of trustees, staff, volunteers, contributors, and organizations that have an interest in the clients. It should be a freestanding committee with the chairperson being someone other than the executive director, although he or she will want to serve as an active member or consultant. Members of the committee should serve staggered terms so that only a portion of them are replaced each year. The committee should write out its own mission statement and conduct business as part of an organization-wide process of improvement. It should have authority and resources to find and eliminate errors in client services, and its actions should be subject only to the full board of trustees.

I am often asked to serve as a consultant to a nonprofit organization's quality improvement committee. I always enjoy meeting with such groups because they typically consist of very enthusiastic and committed people who are close to the organization and want to see it do better if possible. They are usually chosen by someone important, such as the chairman of the board. Those members from outside the staff are well-organized and disciplined individuals who are successful in their own professions. For them to be willing to spend their time helping the organization to improve its delivery of services is in itself an expression of how important the work is perceived to be in the community. The members of the committee usually take their work very seriously and, like myself, feel honored that someone wants to hear their ideas. Because of all these human dynamics, our first meeting is often full of excitement and anticipation.

The meeting usually begins with a couple of short speeches by committee members who express their faith in the organization's mission and the importance of the committee's work. Then, as prearranged, I lecture on the principles of quality so that we can have a common understanding of terms. I begin by describing the benefits of pursuing quality and the way to measure it. Then I explain the definition of quality as conformance to requirements, and the system of quality as prevention, and so on. This group is eager to learn and serious about doing the right thing, so it is only natural for them to want to know what I have found to be the best ways for them to operate and some of the typical quality committee errors. Here is what I tell them.

A common mistake made by quality improvement committees is trying to insulate themselves against bias and conflict of interest by choosing to exclude members of the staff, thinking they might have difficulty criticizing their own work. This puts the committee in the awkward position of asking questions of the people they have deliberately excluded from the committee for reasons of integrity. It is like depending on the inmates to outline the flaws in a prison's security system. They have plenty to lose and nothing to gain. If the staff does not have enough personal integrity to outline the problems objectively as part of the team, what help do you think they will be to an investigating committee? A good mix of staff and volunteers on the committee is very important because they are the ones with process knowledge. If your mission is only to find out what is wrong, you do not need process knowledge. There will always be someone who wants to point out all the errors. Process knowledge allows you to get to the causes of errors so they can be removed forever.

The next most common mistake made by the quality committee is allowing its work to break down into solely a fundraising or public relations effort. The quality improvement committee must focus on the requirements for education and training of the staff and volunteers and the elimination of errors in client services as their highest priorities. It is their job to maintain the quality culture. Reporting the results of the quality improvement process to the public is the job of fund-raisers and public relations staff. Their requirements for information should be included in the committee's work process and, when possible, they should serve as members. But for the pursuit of quality to have its greatest impact on contributors, the organization's story must represent the reality of improved services. In the end, that is what quality management is all about — the open, honest management of reality.

Chapter Review

Whether it is sports, music, the arts, or sciences, our potential to improve is greatly enhanced when we have a desire to learn. The quality leader must be able to kindle the fire of learning in those people he or she wants to lead into quality improvement. Bringing people together in a nonprofit environment to learn new concepts and improve what they are doing will take some premeditation so that the proper sequence of learning events is prescribed.

A successful crusade will have plenty of challenges. To avoid causing unnecessary conflict because of misdirected zeal, take your newfound revelation into the dark recesses of your garage before you spring it on the rest of the world. Test your own commitment to quality improvement by using your energy to bring the maintenance of your car, lawn mower, and paint brushes into conformance with the household's requirements. Once you have brought your garage under control, start through the other subsystems that make your house a home. Target your initial improvement crusade at your own life and personality. Then work with family and friends outside the workplace. You must prove to yourself that you can manage for quality before the message will have a lasting effect on others. *Make a list of some of the household and personal improvements you want to make and describe the price of nonconformance for each one. Then list the requirements for each goal.* Be sure you ask, listen, think, and then do. *Organize the requirements for each goal into processes and procedures, and then prioritize the goals with the easy, short-term goals first and the long-term, more difficult ones last.*

You will have to start working on some of the long-term goals at the same time you begin fulfilling the requirements for some short-term goals. *Check to see which processes can be paired together. Then decide how you will keep track of your progress and measure your performance, and who will help to hold you accountable.*

To bring quality improvement to the forefront of your nonprofit culture, you must create a plan to obtain the total commitment of top management. After you have succeeded at home you can begin to crusade at work. If you are the top manager you can begin to share the concepts of quality management with the members of your board of directors. Take your time and teach them, building each person to the point of commitment. If you are a staff person or volunteer, you can begin by treating your superior as a customer. Win his or her confidence and support by meeting the requirements for your work in extraordinary fashion. Build a reputation for personal quality and wait for your superior to ask about your philosophy and standards. *Write down the requirements for your work. Compare them to the written procedures available. Fill in any gaps by asking your immediate supervisor specific questions about his or her requirements and how you can help fulfill them.*

As you continue your personal growth and improvement efforts, begin to make a list of the most influential people in your organization. It is essential that you be aware of informal structures and politics. Identify the spiritually underemployed true believers. A true believer who is a top manager or a person with significant influence can play a major role in bringing quality management into your culture. Allow your natural relationships with people of influence to provide opportunities to talk about quality management. Do not contrive or manipulate encounters. Allow these things to follow their own course and wait for a quality management subculture to form and solidify. Be patient!

When the opportunity occurs to advance your cause within the top management of your organization, your success will depend greatly upon the research and experience you have had building a subculture. Be ready to provide your listener(s) with a definition of quality, a current assessment of your workplace, and a vision of what it could be. Use examples from your research to capture the attention of your audience. Make your first "moment" short and to the point and ask for the opportunity to continue the discussion in depth. *Begin now to write out what you will say when that moment occurs. Rewrite and practice it regularly.*

If you are the top manager in your organization, you can certainly be much more deliberate in presenting the concepts of quality management to your board and managers than may be reasonable for a staff member or volunteer. However, once an organization has committed to quality management, every staff member and volunteer must receive a quality education. Everyone in the organization must own the concepts individually. The process of education must be continuous and include considerations for new staff members and volunteers as well as reviewing concepts with the once-educated.

A quality improvement committee should be appointed to oversee the pursuit of quality, maintain quality awareness, implement educational and training initiatives, routinely eliminate errors, and hold the organization accountable for performance. The committee should include members from your board, staff, volunteers, contributors, and other members of the community. It will be their job to encourage and maintain the quality culture. *Begin now to make a list of those people you think should serve on your quality improvement committee.*

References

Crosby, P. B. *Quality Is Free.* New York: McGraw-Hill, 1979.

Crosby, P. B. *Quality Without Tears.* New York: McGraw-Hill, 1984.

Crosby, P. B. *The Patterns of Quality Troubles.* Winter Park, Fla.: Philip Crosby Associates, 1985.

Index